TRIGGER WARNING

Life with Multiple Identities

Thank you!

♡ A. Rose

By Annika Rose

ANNIKA ROSE

TRIGGER WARNING

ANNIKA ROSE

DISCLAIMER

The topics in this book can be quite distressing to read.
If you are feeling triggered or otherwise dysregulated, please close the
book and take care of yourself. Your mental health is far more important
than finishing this book in any given amount of time.

This book is based on true events. It reflects the author's present
recollections of experiences over time. Some names and characteristics have
been changed, some events have been compressed, and some dialogue has
been recreated to protect the privacy of the people involved.

ANNIKA ROSE

ACKNOWLEDGMENT

A special thanks to my support system, biological family, chosen family, friends, and mental health care providers who have helped me face my demons and write my experiences. This process has been so healing and I have been able to move toward living a happy, healthy, productive life because of it.

A special shout out to my social media family. You all have been the cheerleading section of this process and I honestly don't know if I would have kept pushing forward with writing had it not been for your encouragement and support.

ANNIKA ROSE

How Did We Get Here?

"As traumatized children, we always dreamed that someone would come and save us. We never dreamed that it would, in fact, be ourselves as adults." – Alice Little

My name is Annika Rose, and I am an alter in a body that has Dissociative Identity Disorder. While I am the author, you will notice that "Hailey" is referred to throughout the book. That is the name that our system goes by in public, as it is the given name of the body.

I am writing this book along with the other alters in our system in order to educate about this disorder, and to validate those that live with it.

As a child, fear was our operating system. During our first memorable trauma I was told by my abuser that the trauma was my fault and that my mom would stop loving me if I told her what had happened. From then on, and throughout my life, I have struggled to vocalize what hurts me, what I feel may hurt others, or what could potentially cause real or perceived abandonment. I still needed to communicate, so I wrote about these things. I journaled, I wrote letters, I joined writing competitions, and eventually became an author.

Children that are programmed with fear crave safety and protection. They need the connection of someone who will believe them and validate where they have been and where they are going.

I began writing my trauma timeline in 2014 when I was first diagnosed with dissociative identity disorder. In 2016 I used that timeline in narrative therapy to write my trauma story in more detail. After 5 years, and having forgotten that I had written my trauma timeline, I was knee deep in therapy for dissociative identity disorder. When I remembered that I had all of the words on paper, I was moved to turn that trauma story into a book about life with DID, including what I went through, how I learned to cope with an overwhelming amount of trauma, and how I'm able to move forward.

This is likely the hardest piece of work that I have written to date. Each of my alters had to revisit the very traumas that created them, and we all had to face feelings of abandonment, sadness, anger, anxiety, loneliness, and frustration.

The most difficult part of writing this book, however, was the self-gaslighting that I experienced. Thoughts flooded my mind, "*What if I'm making this all up?*", "*What if I'm just delusional?*", "*What if no one believes me?*".

As it turns out, this is a common phenomenon in people with DID – we have been so gaslighted in our past that we start to question our own memories and sanity. Each time a thought comes up it is important that I challenge it. I remember that this is my story, that no one else has walked in my shoes, and that it would be impossible to fake something so consistently for years on end.

This is all to say that we got to this point via much insight, many hours behind a computer, a whole lot of therapy, and keeping in the forefront the goal of creating a piece of work that is not only engaging, but also educational.

What Is DID?

Dissociative Identity Disorder was previously known as Multiple Personality Disorder. The name was changed in the nineties due to the fact that it is not a personality disorder, rather it is a dissociative disorder caused by severe childhood trauma.

DID is internationally recognized and is classified both in the International Classification of Diseases – 10th edition (ICD-10), and in the Diagnostic and Statistical Manual of Mental Disorders – 5th Edition (DSM-V).

In the ICD-10, DID bears a diagnosis code of F44.81 and is defined as:

Dissociative Identity Disorder (aka Multiple Personality Disorder)

A disorder characterized by the presence of two or more identities with distinct patterns of perception and personality which recurrently take control of the person's behavior; this is accompanied by a retrospective gap in memory of important personal information that far exceeds ordinary forgetfulness. The changes in identity are not due to substance use or to a general medical condition.

A dissociative disorder in which the individual adopts two or more distinct personalities. Each personality is a fully integrated and complex unit with memories, behavior patterns and social friendships. Transition from one personality to another is sudden.

There are multiple theories as to how DID develops, but the one most commonly adopted is "The Theory of Structural Dissociation" initially introduced in the book "The Haunted Self: Structural Dissociation and the Treatment of Chronic Traumatization" by Onno van der Hart, Ellert Nijenjuis, and Kathy Steele.

This theory posits that nobody is born with a solidified personality, rather we are born with collection of different ego states that eventually come together to create a singular personality around the ages of 6-9. For people with DID, severe childhood trauma disrupts this integration process and blocks the ability to integrate those ego states, causing those states to group separately into multiple 'selves'.

I like to think of it as the components of a cake. We are all born with the makings of one cake: flour, sugar, vanilla, shortening, etc. In a person without DID, all of these ingredients begin to mingle and combine throughout childhood until the body is about 6-9 years old, and voila, one full cake. For a person with DID, we are born with the same ingredients, but severe trauma puts our ingredients in different cupboards which interrupts the mixing process and makes it so that we have different groups of ingredients by the age of 6-9 instead of one cake.

While the diagnostic criteria remain the same, it is important to know that each person with DID is very different. We all experienced different types of traumas, have had different support structures, and have gone through development differently.

The differences can range from the amount of alters that someone has, to the co-occurring disorders they may struggle with, to their gender identity, and more.

One thing that does stay fairly consistent are the terms used in the DID community.

System: the collection of all the alters that exist in one brain.

Alters: The 'personalities' that make up the system. (These can be called a myriad of things such as 'parts', 'head mates', and 'identities', among others.)

Host: The alter that identifies with the body and goes by the body's government name (usually), in a broader sense, it is the alter that is in control of the body the most.

Front: The alter that is in control of the body at any given time.

Dissociative Amnesia: the memory loss that exists between different alters.

Co-Conscious: when two or more alters are fronting at the same time (the dissociative amnesia between the fronting alters is minimal at this point)

If you think of it as a pie: the system is the whole pie, and the alters are the pieces of pie – each one separated by different degrees of dissociative amnesia.

In my system, we call our alters, 'parts', and each part is completely individual and unique. Each part has their own likes, dislikes, preferences, memories, social structures, talents, roles, handwriting, voice inflections, body language, triggers, goals, etc.

You will notice that sometimes I refer to myself with singular language, and sometimes with plural language. "I" will be used when a certain alter is talking about their own reality, and "Us/We" will be used when we are referring to the whole system. We are currently writing this book about our system; this is to say that multiple alters are writing this book together. Sometimes the pronouns change and are inconsistent, and that is simply because we are writing a book about DID while having DID.

I have lived with dissociative identity disorder since early childhood but was not diagnosed until I turned 30. I knew something was different about me since the age of 12, but I had no communication with, or knowledge of, my other parts. There have been clinicians earlier in my adulthood that had illuded to the possibility of me having DID, but it never became a definitive diagnosis.

When I was eventually diagnosed, I was devastated. I was positive that I would never be loved again, because after all, I am crazy, right? Now, as I have lived with the knowledge of the disorder, I have come to believe that DID is one of the most creative ways that a person's brain can make sense of situations that just simply don't make sense.

While the disorder began in early childhood, and some core parts were created in childhood, the creation of alters did not end there. People with DID continue to gain alters as they age and experience other traumas. Throughout the book I will reference times where I felt a bath of ice run through my veins, experienced foggy thinking, and the sensation of being pulled backward. That is what it feels like when my brain copes by making a new alter. This doesn't happen simply by getting stressed out, rather it happens when my nervous system gets so overwhelmed that it cannot cope in the state that we are at in that moment.

We are excited to share this information with you, and the best way to do that is to tell you our story, so without further ado, here it is.

TRIGGER WARNING

Life with Multiple Identities

By: Annika Rose

ANNIKA ROSE

Stolen Innocence

Age 4

I'm standing on my tippy toes reaching over the green tiled bathroom counter, my little fingers splashed in the running water when Jim, my stepdad, came in. I lived with him and my biological mom in a small apartment on Chicago's south side. My mom had gone to run an errand, and I was left with him, alone.

He looked down at me and said, "I was in a fire and I was hurt, do you think you could help me feel better?"

I stepped back from the sink and looked up at him. Being the carefree 4-year-old that I was, I eagerly agreed. His face flushed and his eyes got dark.

I can still hear the clink of the belt he was wearing as he unfastened it, the woosh of the zipper, and the weight of his trousers as they hit the floor, pooling around his tree trunk ankles. His blue patterned cotton boxer shorts were wrinkled, fresh out of the Kmart packaging. He pulled them down to his mid thighs, exposing himself to me.

I was aware that this was a private part. My stomach began to churn with anxiety and confusion.

"I need to put a special bandage on it, but when I'm done, I need you to kiss my owie."

While I waited for him to put the see-through balloon over his wound, my body grew cold and numb and the room got blurry. My eyes hyper focused on the sink vanity that was to my left and the faucet which was at eye level. The

17

edge of the counter had rounded tiles, smooth, with crumbling grey grout holding them in place. The reflection of his sweaty face was in the round mirror that hung above us as he looked down at his bandage.

He finished 'wrapping himself' and presented his penis to my small face. He instructed me and I kissed his booboo as directed. My vision remained fixated on the counter tiles. My tummy told me that this was a bad thing and my nervous system was flooded with confusion. I felt myself float away, mentally hiding in the clawfoot tub that was to the right of me.

Click, click, the apartment door unlocked.

His body stiffened and a look of panic washed over him as the front door to the apartment opened and I heard the soothing voice of my mother.

"Hey guys, I'm back!"

She had just returned from the grocery store and was headed for the kitchen.

He quickly pulled up his pants and aggressively sat me down on the toilet behind me. His lumbering body leaned over me. I could smell the ranch dressing that was lingering on his breath as he said,

"Don't you tell your mother about this. You are a bad girl, and if she knew, she wouldn't love you anymore. Stay here until I tell you to come out."

I curled up on the floor, hugging my knees to my chest with my back to the steel coiled register. I was terrified to make a noise, terrified of being found.

Shortly thereafter, my mom, who was not aware of the abuse, began to notice that something was off with Jim and knew that she had to make a gut-wrenching decision for my welfare. She recognized that my biological dad could provide a better life for me financially, so she chose to transfer my care to him and his wife Jennifer.

Subconsciously I had put two and two together. Jim said my mom would stop loving me if she found out about what I did, and then my mom gave me to my dad.

Was it my fault that she left? Did she find out?

Unfortunately, as a tiny human, I was unable to parse out why any of these things were happening. It all felt like abandonment, and I internalized each event and misassigned the fault to myself.

I didn't realize when she dropped me off that she would only be in my life sporadically from then on, but I got into a routine and began to get used to my new reality little by little.

~~~

In life, I have found that there are 'intentional traumas' and 'unintentional traumas', and within those, are events that may be traumatic for one person, but not for another.

Jim molesting me at the age of 4 was an 'intentional trauma'. He knew what he was doing was wrong and he did it anyway. This would have been a trauma for anyone that had gone through it.

This trauma was the first time that I remember dissociating to survive an event. It's something that my brain learned to do to keep me safe, and it would become a common reaction as traumatic events persisted in my early childhood.

My mom giving me to my dad was an 'unintentional trauma'. She did not mean to hurt me when she made that decision. She was doing the best she could with what she had at the time. As an adult, I can appreciate these 'rock and a hard place' dilemmas. This may not have been a trauma to some people, but for me it was.

ANNIKA ROSE

A New Foundation

Age 5

I had lived with my Dad and Jennifer for a couple of months in rural Iowa when I met my new neighbor friends, Amber and Autumn. I was 5 years old, and they were 7 and 8 years old respectively. They lived right down the hill from our 2-bedroom farm house. We spent the whole summer together.

Amber and Autumn did not come from a safe home. I do not know the extent of the abuse, but I know that I was not allowed to go down to their house, ever. They only knew one way to live, and unfortunately, their upbringing deeply impacted my life.

Because I could not go down to their house, it was not uncommon for their little faces to pop up in our living room picture window accompanied by knocks,

"Can Hailey come out to playyyyy?"

My cousins who babysat me were more than happy to have me out of the house while they danced around the living room to Cyndi Lauper playing on the record player.

Thirty feet behind the house, to the south, were rows upon rows of corn, which was knee high by the fourth of July – on a good year. While we played in the back yard, we often ventured into the field.

"Let's play house!" Amber squealed.

"Hailey, you are the mom, but you have to change clothes."

I hesitated, "But, I don't have any other clothes."

They insisted that I pretend, "Go deeper into the corn and take your clothes off and lay down in the dirt like you haven't woken up yet… then we will come wake you up."

Being self-conscious and new to playing alone with friends, I did as they suggested. I heard distant giggles which quickly trailed off. I lay there for what seemed like an hour.

Fear welled up in my gut, *they aren't coming back*. Panicked and alone, I quickly wiggled back into my clothes and started running down the row, cutting my legs and arms on the leaves of the stalks that towered over me.

Upon entering the house, my cousins had hardly noticed that I was gone, but did notice how dirty I had become.

"Your dad is going to be pissed, go clean yourself off".

I went to wash off the dirt and humiliation. This wouldn't be the last time that my friends would play in this manner.

Toward the end of the summer, as usual, Amber and Autumn came over to play in the afternoon. I am not sure where my cousins were, but it was just us three in the back of the house.

Autumn suggested, "Let's play cops and robbers, and you are caught, and we have to tie you up so you don't get away!"

Panic filled my stomach, but desperate for companionship, I sat down on the vinyl seat of the kitchen chair which was dragged into my dad's bedroom. They opened the closet door to my right pulling out the tie hanger that was on my dad's side.

"I'm not supposed to play with anything in here…" I pleaded with them to choose something else to tie me up with.

They ignored me, littering the floor with my dad's ties and belts. First, my legs. Belts fusing mine and the chair's legs into one.

Oh, this is okay, it's just my legs, I rationalized internally.

Then Autumn went behind me and used the thick belts donning western belt buckles to secure my small torso, arms at my sides, to the back of the chair. I began to feel fuzzy and cold – like when Jim had me in the bathroom not long ago.

"Should we put a tie over her mouth and nose?" Autumn asked Amber.

"No, that would make her die", she responded.

"So? We would just leave and no one would know it was us…".

I am unsure if they ever did cover my mouth and nose because mentally, I went into the furthest corner of the room to remove myself from these sadistic children.

The next thing I remember was the sound of tires on the gravel driveway. They panicked and I was left scrambling to get free from, and re-organize my dad's items.

I made sure that no one knew what happened. I feared what would happen if my dad found out. He is a large man, towering over me with a body like a linebacker. His shouts scared me and I couldn't help but burst out crying when he was upset.

"If you don't stop crying, I'll give you something to cry about." A common threat.

At that time, I did not know if he was telling the truth or fibbing.

Nights were terrifying. Dad and Jennifer slept in their room across the hall with their door shut. Paralyzed by the fear of making noise or doing anything without permission, I sat on the floor outside of their door every night scared to upset them, but also scared to use the bathroom. I would finally work up the courage to open the door.

"Um Jennifer… Jennifer?"

"Yes Hailey, what?"

Sensing the irritation in her tone, I quickly ask, "Can I use the bathroom?"

Exasperated she consistently replied, "Yes Hailey, you can, you don't have to ask me

every night."

Once permission was given, I would sneak across the hallway to the bathroom to relieve myself, quickly finishing and hopping back into bed.

Despite the fears that I was consumed with and the situations I had already been subjected to, I had a side that was always delighted, always full of light and joy. I was in awe of the things around me, animals especially.

One day I was playing in my bedroom, Jennifer was folding clothes and putting them away in my closet.

"Hailey, you know what?"

"Huh?" I said half listening.

With an air of excitement, she responded "You are going to have a little sister. She's in

my belly!"

I was going to have a little sister!

Conscientious as I was, I asked her a few days later, "Jenny?",

"Yes Hailey"

"Since I'm going to have a little sister, do you think I should call you mommy just so she

doesn't get confused?"

She looked down at me with love in her eyes, "Yes, Hailey, I would like that."

From then on, she was mommy to me.

In the evenings, Jennifer would tuck me into my single bed with my stuffed animals. My toy box was at the foot of the bed and my dresser was against the far wall. A small window on the right let the corn stalks look in on the small room.

In order to fend off the nightmares, she would lead me in my nighttime prayer as I drifted off to sleep.

Now I lay me down to sleep

I pray the Lord my soul to keep

If I die before I wake

I pray the Lord my soul to take.

God bless Mommy and Daddy and Mommy and Emma and Kristy and Mary and Hailey, and alllllll the toys in my toybox.

Uprooted

Ages 6-7

Shortly after Jennifer gave birth to Savannah, our family moved to a 3-bedroom townhome in another state. It wasn't long before my uncle, aunt, and their 3 kids moved in with us. Four adults, 3 teens, a 6-year-old and an infant?? This was a recipe for chaos.

A year into our move, Jennifer had another baby, Jason. I felt lost in the movement of the family and locations. I was completely knocked off my center and further away from my biological mom than I ever had been. I was afraid to make noise, afraid to be a "better door than a window", afraid to exist.

I was proud to be an older sister again, and I loved helping with dishes, baby stuff, and taking care of the babies. With all the commotion in the house, the connection that I desired became more elusive. I began to throw myself off my bed at night to get either of my parents to come upstairs to check on me, to no avail.

Evenings were spent in front of the large, wood encased television. I often acted as the remote control, changing the channels and adjusting the volume per my dad's requests. "Rescue 911" and "M.A.S.H." were the evening routine. At times, he could be impatient, his brow furrowing in the middle and his tone was gruffer.

I always felt that I was in trouble and the shame that was planted at 4 years old began to grow. I worked hard to please my family by staying out of the way, cleaning, doing well in school, and advancing in my extracurriculars. Looking back now, I realize that I was more afraid of my dad than the other kids were because I had been threatened by a man before, and in my experience, the threat came to fruition, my biological mom found out about the abuse and left. I was terrified of being abandoned again, and there was no one else after my dad to take care of me. I believed him when he threatened to make me cry, and I was terrified to make him mad.

I continued to crave belonging and love. I craved a mother figure. My dad's wife was nice and all, but she was not the nurturer that I needed.

I spent a lot of time playing outside the townhomes, biking, playing pretend, and eventually meeting our neighbors, Lydia and Marshall. They were in their early fifties and lived 3 doors down from our townhome. They often sat in their garage, chain smoking and giving dumdum suckers to the children of the neighborhood. They took an interest in me, asking me questions about my likes and dislikes, eventually inviting me into their home.

I walked into their dimly lit living room, hit in the face with cigarette smoke and lingering ammonia from an unattended litter box. Before my parents became concerned, Lydia and Marshall took precautions. They introduced themselves to my family, interrupting any weird vibes that may have been subconsciously festering.

I remember trusting Lydia.

She began to ask me questions about my parents, very specific questions. "Does your daddy spank you when he is angry?"

"Would you like to come live with us?"

The couple seemed to care so much for me. They even let me take a bath at their home when I was muddy from playing outdoors. For some reason, they liked to take pictures of me while I was in the bathtub, it was our secret.

On a cold spring day, I was too excited to wait for summer and successfully convinced my dad to pull my bike out of the garage. As I repetitively rode up and down the sidewalk, I noticed my dad talking to someone I didn't know, but who looked very 'official'.

Lydia came out of her apartment, which was right behind me. She stood with her hands on my shoulders as my dad talked to the person. I strained to hear what was being said. His eyes were lasers, settling on me with an anger I hadn't seen before. The discourse continued until my dad shook their hand and they left.

He pointed to me and ordered me in the house. Lydia hesitated, and then let go of my shoulders whispering "It's going to be okay; I promise."

What was going to be okay?

Once in the house, dad sat me down and forbade me from seeing Lydia and Marshall.

"What did you tell them?"

I had no idea what he was talking about.

"Did you tell them that I hit you??"

My heart was beating in my head, pulsing with fear. I racked my brain, reviewing every answer that I had given to the couple's barrage of questions.

"No, I don't think so... I mean, they asked if you spanked me, but everyone gets spanked when they are bad, right?"

His face grew red, "Don't you EVER tell people what goes on in this house."

My face was sunburned with shame.

"The police were called on me because Marshall was under the impression that I was beating you. The police could have taken you away and you wouldn't have seen any of us again."

The tears stung as I willed them to stay behind my eyelids, he didn't like when I cried. I knew I could never speak with Lydia and Marshall again. They had called social services and I was in a lot of trouble.

Eventually, my aunt, uncle, and cousins moved down the hill to an apartment of their own.

During the two short years that we lived there, I got in trouble for lying multiple times. I was accused of many things that I was positive I did not do. Offenses ranged from stealing candy from the class guessing jar to stealing candy from the store all the way to going further down the street than allowed. I had no memory of anything I was accused of, so I denied it, however, they were convinced that I was lying. I was positive that I did not do the things I was being accused of. Nevertheless, I spent a lot of my childhood trying to justify myself, only to end up grounded despite my efforts.

These conflicts were the first signs that I had dissociative identity disorder. Hindsight being 20/20, it is now clear to me that the 'lying' wasn't untruth, it was that another alter was committing the offenses that I had no memory of.

ANNIKA ROSE

Secrets

Age 8

In the summer between second and third grade, I along with my siblings were babysat by Barb. She was a tall heavyset woman with dark shoulder length hair. Savannah, Jason, and I spent our time in and around her three-story home. It had a dark basement and a small attic, both of which I would become intimately acquainted with. During the school year, I went to her house afterward to wait for my parents. During the summer, I spent the whole day under her watch.

Barb had it out for me from the get-go it seemed. Before school, my little sister Savannah, little brother Jason, and I watched morning cartoons until it was time for me to walk the few blocks to the elementary school. One day, we were sitting on the couch watching tv. I was on the far-left side of the couch and Barb left Jason laying on the far-right side. He was only about a year old. I was immersed in the show we were watching when Jason rolled off the couch creating a *thud*.

"What the FUCK were you thinking you fat asshole?? Do you just not CARE about your brother?!" She was livid.

I felt so bad because I couldn't have gotten to him before he fell even if I *had* noticed he was rolling off the couch, which I didn't. I was blamed for failing to catch him. I was seven. Her proclivity for finding fault in me was impressive.

Summers were hot and muggy. Walking outside guaranteed a drenching of sweat. Barb had gotten a slip-n-slide for the daycare kids to enjoy in the backyard. She took me to the kitchen and pointed to a white square device.

"Step up on it."

I didn't know what it was, but she was insistent. I hesitated.

She pushed me, more firmly, "Get. On. It."

She weighed me at a plump 82 pounds.

While cackling, she said snidely "You are too much of a fatty for this, you would rip it and ruin it for all the rest of the kids. You can watch."

I was put on my first diet under her care. During lunches, I got half of a sandwich when the other kids got a whole sandwich. She weighed me regularly, laughing at me with her son, Jared, who was often in the room. When the other children snacked, I ran laps around the perimeter of her house.

While she was definitely bad, she didn't hold a candle to Jared who handled my punishments. They ranged from being locked in the attic, to being forced to watch horror films in the dark, to sexual abuse in the basement.

When he would lead me up the stairs to the bathroom, I knew he was going to shove me through the small hatch that entered into the attic. It was sweltering in the summer; fiberglass particles scratched my skin as I looked out the small window down onto the street. As unpleasant as it was, this was my safe space. This is the place I would go in my mind when other abuses were happening.

At the end of each abuse, Jared would remind me that no one would believe me if I told them what was happening, and that I would get into more trouble if my parents found out. I acquiesced and followed his flawed logic. It was our secret.

On the few occasions that I tried to tell my parents about my fears, it was shot down because she had already convinced them that I was untrustworthy. That was until one day when they picked the three of us up, gathered the kid's toys in a white laundry basket, and said that was the last time we'd be there. I don't know why they decided to do it now, but I wasn't going to complain.

The Odd Duck

Ages 9-12

The summer ended with a move to a nearby town. We had our own house!! Upstairs were the kitchen, living room, a bathroom, and two bedrooms, and downstairs there were 3 other bedrooms, a huge playroom, and a laundry room. The yard was so big that when we eventually got a golden lab, we were able to play with him without a street being too close by.

I began the 3rd grade at the local K-5 school, which was not lacking in challenges. I was teased relentlessly. I'm almost certain that I was an odd duck, absent minded and often distracted. I was teased for my height and my build, which was not slight.

In 4th grade, while in math class, one of the popular girls had to leave class to go to the bathroom in the middle of a quiz, and then another one of the popular girls had to go, so the teacher got a bit impatient.

"Miss... Miss..." I tried to get the teacher's attention.

In a hushed tone she acknowledged me, "Hailey, we are taking a quiz."

"Please, I need to go to the bathroom, really bad." I pleaded with her.

Assuming that the other two were cheating, she was not about to let me go to the bathroom. What she didn't know was that I had a bladder infection and couldn't hold it for long.

I begged 3 times to go to the bathroom and she got mad and started to ignore my pleas. Not long into her lesson on fractions, I stood up with my legs crossed and looked at her with tears streaming down my cheeks,

"I couldn't hold it, I'm so sorry, I'm so sorry!!!" My light jeans began to grow dark down the front.

I was mortified, and the class laughed.

The teaching assistant walked me through the cafeteria where all of the big kids (5th graders) were eating, we passed the library, and went into the nurse's office. Luckly the school kept extra clothes for situations just like this. I continued to cry and I wished I could disappear.

When I left school that day, my new daycare provider noticed my new pants.

"What did you do, pee your pants?"

She was kidding, but I started crying all over again.

She was a good daycare lady, she was my friend Sarah's mom, and we got to play in the basement with all of her mom's Mary Kay makeup.

Fifth grade was the last year of elementary school, so the teachers started to prepare us for the move to the new middle school. This was also the year that the schools started to do health screenings. They took our height, weight, and a measurement of our spine to test for scoliosis. When it came my turn, I took off my shoes and stepped onto the scale.

The volunteer mom that was taking the measurements laughed and looked at the nurse, "Well this one is sure hefty."

I was so ashamed. I don't think it would have been so bad if we were in the privacy of the nurse's office, but we weren't, we were in the 5th grade hallway, and my whole class was waiting in line behind me. My biggest insecurity was being reinforced in front of 30 of my peers.

Moving into the middle school was an adventure, one in which I would learn how cruel kids can be. Grade 6 is when we had to start running "the mile" which was 4 laps around our asphalt track, or 15 laps around the inside of the gym. Anxiety turned into exhaustion, exhaustion morphed into defeat, and when everyone had reached the finish line, I was just starting my final lap with tears streaming down my face. I could hear the exasperated sighs from my classmates, and I could feel the frustration from the gym teacher, a man in his 50's, shorter than me, with a beer belly and a clip board.

Mortified at the 'huge' body I was convinced that I had, I would finish the mile run with an asthma induced wheeze which would cause me to cough for the rest of the school day.

If only I was skinnier, I would fit in, I would be able to run the mile, I would be liked.

I spent summers with my biological mom in Kansas City. She had a small blue house with 2 bedrooms. She rented out the downstairs apartment to my sister, who was in law school. At the top of the dead-end street were a few horses in a large pasture. The gates that held them in were wide enough for me to pet their soft noses, and to bond with them in a way I hadn't been able to with my peers. Diamond was black with a white diamond on her forehead, and Toot was named after his horrid flatulence.

I told my new animal friends about my life, about the abuse, the bullying, and the exploitation. They supported me and came to the fence whenever I showed up. I could rely on them and I found security in their support.

The summer before 8th grade, I was at my mom's house when I felt my chin go numb. I looked in the small mirror hanging above the stove and noticed the left side of my face begin to droop and eventually stop working. I tried to go to the couch, but up felt like down, left felt like right, and my head met the corner of the coffee table.

I called my mom at work, "Um, mom, my face isn't working and I'm really dizzy. I fell."

She was immediately concerned that I had had a heat stroke and she raced home. The next thing I remember, I was in a small curtained off stall in an emergency room. Everything felt surreal, like I was watching it on a movie. They diagnosed me with Bell's Palsy, a neurological condition that they didn't have much understanding of at the time. Prognosis: it could be months or years before I got control of my face again. Luckily, my face started to heal just shortly before the eighth grade started.

All of my peers were curious about what had happened to my face. They were being nice; they were concerned about me. It was a nice reprieve. I patiently explained that it was something with my nerves and that it would go away.

Eventually the novelty wore off and they used my drooping face to ramp up their alienation of me. Calling someone a "Palsy" was the new insult to describe kids with special needs.

The nurse's office started to see me more often, and when I wasn't there, I was hiding in a bathroom stall. Nowhere was safe.

I vividly remember walking home from school one afternoon when I noticed a voice in my head,

"Someday you will find that you are different from other people. You have something no one else does, and you will find out what that is later, but not today."

It was at this time that I felt life becoming 2D. Everything seemed flat. I felt alienated and alone, despite the fact that I was involved in a lot of programs and looked like an outgoing middle school girl. My inner world and perceptions were vastly different than my outward presentation.

Growing Pains

Age 13-15

I transitioned to high school after my 13th birthday. I was anxious and self-conscious and this was the first time that I was terrified of people seeing me.

I was very involved in my church and was excited about the newness of everything. It was a fresh start, new pens, new paper, new trapper keeper; a new me (quite literally). I found refuge in the music department at school. It was the place I felt the safest, and the place that I developed most as a teenaged human.

My best friend talked me into trying out for cheerleading with her. I did it to support her, never expecting that they would choose me. To my surprise, I was added to the wrestling cheerleading team. Our workouts were tough for me at first as I wasn't very active before that. There were times that I would have to stop to catch my breath, and I couldn't keep up with the smaller girls on the team. I was also battling a very painful ankle. I worked so hard to learn the cheers for the meets and practiced more than most of the girls on the squad, which seemed futile since I still couldn't do the splits and struggled to get a lot of height in my jumps.

One day, the coaches and team captains called Jennifer in to have a conference. They accused me of cheating on my workouts and talked about how my weight was affecting my performance. They said that I was on probation, and that I couldn't do certain jumps until I had lost some weight and proved to them that I was really committed.

I was mortified. I went home and cried for hours and frantically tried to figure out how to lose weight. I walked into the kitchen where Jennifer was cleaning the fridge out. I rested my chin on the top of the refrigerator door and told her I really wanted to lose weight.

She was distracted and mindlessly responded, "If you want it so bad, do something about it."

I am positive she did not mean that I should go to the lengths that I did shortly thereafter.

From early fall until mid-spring, I became friends with two seniors that were in choir with me. One of them was very skinny and her breath smelled like peppermint covered vomit. She was always chewing gum and her teeth were clearly rotting. The taller of the two was thin, but her breath wasn't as bad, though her skin was dry and flaky. They took me in and eventually taught me how to lose weight like they did. Throughout the year, I restricted food by throwing away my breakfast after a few bites, and by skipping lunch at school. If I had eaten more than 1 or two bites, I purged in the bathroom, the door guarded by a friend.

Near the end of 9th grade, our choir took a trip to Chicago. My two choir friends introduced me to diet pills and showed me where to find them in a health food store. They said it was easier than throwing everything up that I ate. I gave them a try, but they made me sicker to my stomach.

I vowed that I would be exactly what my cheerleading coaches wanted by the end of the summer. My plan was perfect. Jennifer and Dad worked away from home, so I would have the whole day to myself. Even when I visited my biological mom, I was unattended when she was at work. The plan was to work out every day, eat "healthy", and purge what food I did eat.

Four days before the end of the school year, we went out as a family, having dinner at a restaurant and going to a movie afterward. The restaurant didn't have the salad that I was planning on and I panicked.

What is easy to get rid of? What do I do now??

I ended up ordering a hot ham and cheese sandwich meal. When the food came to the table, I picked at it while the rest of my family ate normally. I took about 3 bites as my anxiety turned to panic.

I'm not going to be able to get rid of this... what do I do??

I excused myself to the bathroom. Moments later, Jennifer walked in and saw my feet were pointing to the wall.

Firmly she said, "What the hell are you doing?"

"I'm, I'm undoing my belt…" I was wholly unbelievable.

I was busted. Through clenched teeth she demanded, "Get out here, wash your hands, and meet me back at the table."

My parents were livid and went into damage control mode. Before I knew it, I was sitting in a small waiting room of an eating disorder clinic. Body positive posters and artwork made by patients of the clinic hung on the walls.

"Hailey?…" A short woman holding a clipboard called my name.

I felt my body slowly rise and follow her. The doctor had me sit on the cold grey table facing her. My parents sat in the chairs along the wall staring intently at the doctor. She grabbed my hands and looked at my fingers and fingernails, pointing out to my parents the rough appearance of my right middle finger in comparison to the others. She explained what 'bulimia' was, how serious it is, and the consequences of living with it.

I went to that clinic weekly for the summer, learning about eating disorders and apparently getting 'healed'.

I turned 14 during the summer, and when it came time to go back to school, we all assumed that because I didn't have the symptoms anymore that it was okay for me to start cheerleading again. I stopped going to treatment. I continued to restrict, though I didn't purge anymore. Between classes, friends, cheerleading, drama club, choir, and youth group, I wasn't home much. I was okay with that.

Our family participated in diet after diet - Atkins and Herbalife being the main themes, so it was easy for me to restrict and exercise to lose weight because my family was in diet mindset.

As I tried to escape what I felt was chaos, I became friends with the girl across the street. She was 17. We were in her bedroom one afternoon watching MTV when she said we should play 'house'. She said she was going to be the dad and I was going to be the mom. A little put off, but curious, I agreed. We reenacted male and female gender roles, and then she kissed me. Her braces were sharp against my lips. I was frozen. I quietly said I didn't know if I wanted to play anymore. Pushing me down on her twin mattress she laid on top of me, pinning my arms and legs together and continued to kiss me. Her tongue assaulted my mouth as tears streamed down the sides of my face, wetting my hair and her pillow. When she decided she was done, she said no one could know.

That was the last time I hung out with her, but I had another secret that I had to keep, once again, no one could know.

As school continued, Jennifer noticed that I never needed more lunch money. She worked with the school and started checking the records of what I would order. Now that 'big brother' was watching, I began to order normal meals, would eat a couple bites, cover the rest with napkins, and slide the remnants into the garbage.

In the winter of 10th grade, my church youth group, Jennifer, and I went to a Christian conference geared toward teenagers in Fargo, ND. This conference was the first place that I had heard of broken homes, and that they were common. I felt so reassured that I wasn't alone, that other people didn't have their biological mom and dad in the same home, and that they felt the same loneliness and longing that I did. They went on to explain that God could adopt us into His family if we just accept and follow Jesus. I was craving that belonging, I could taste it.

At the end, they had an altar call, asking anyone who hadn't 'accepted Christ' to come forward, as well as those who wanted prayer regarding their homelife. I went down, even though I thought I might be hurting Jennifer's feelings.

I was placed in a group of about 4 girls and was taken to a spot to sit down with an adult woman. We each shared our stories and she explained to us how our sins damned us to hell, but by 'accepting Christ', we would be saved from that damnation and adopted into God's family.

Cries echoed throughout the mezzanine as the teens recognized their 'sins' and begged for forgiveness. The teenage grief floated in the air like a haze. The chaperones of the small groups prayed while we cried. Without what they were offering, I was doomed to hell and that is NOT what I wanted. I wanted to be adopted into the family of God, where I was promised a loving family that could never break. I accepted Christ into my heart and pledged to follow Him for the rest of my life. It wasn't until much later that I realized how manipulative and damaging these experiences were.

The Christianity that I grew up with was focused largely on the book of Revelation. I learned that the end times were coming and that I had to examine my heart and mind for anything bad because Jesus will come like a "thief in the night", and it would be bad to be caught up in anything nefarious when that happens. I was convinced that I was irreparably flawed, and anything less than perfection wasn't okay.

During my teenage years, my parent's relationship was strained. I tried to bring peace to the house by cleaning, getting A's, staying out of the way, and agreeing with everything. The fear of disappointing them swallowed me.

Despite my efforts, I was a straight B student, people pleaser, over-booked, anxious, and depressed teenager. I was bullied for my naivety, my faith, and my proclivity for having crushes on pretty much every guy in school. I wanted so badly to be loved and to be shown affection.

Around this time, my dad had finished seminary, and the need to make him look good in public by being an ideal kid became overwhelming. I began to spend a lot of time at school, mostly in the music department organizing music in large grey filing cabinets.

I had completed most of my credits by my junior year and I was known for being attentive, efficient, and compliant. I was also known to 'daydream' in class – something that drove my calculus teacher crazy. I would stare out the window, nothing going on in my head, just escaping. After a while, I was able to schedule my whole afternoon with study halls so I could work on things that didn't require much focused attention.

Everyone has that one teacher that made a major impact on their life. Ms. Hansen was that teacher for me. She really saw me. She encouraged my singing and helped me realize that I was not as defective as I had previously determined. I spent many afternoons crying on the floor of her office purely because I felt so lonely and exhausted. She went about her business during those times, handing me tissues and placing a sympathetic hand on my shoulder every now and then. She believed in me and nurtured the part of me that really needed to be seen.

I didn't realize at the time how important this safe space would be moving forward.

ANNIKA ROSE

Disclosure

Age 16

I began to have vivid and recurrent nightmares which eventually leaked into the daytime as flashbacks. These were happening for a year before I told anyone. That was until I was visiting with my biological mom in the back yard of my grandfather's townhome.

"Can I talk to you about something?" I played with the hem of my shirt looking down for fear she would reject me.

"Of course," she said as she took a drag of her Pall Mall cigarette.

Hesitantly, I approached, "So, I've been having nightmares and these memories during the day about something that happened when I was really young."

"Mhmm" she hummed patiently.

"Was the bathroom in the Chicago apartment to the right of the living room when you come in the front door?"

"Yes" her suspicion started to increase.

"And was there older tile in the bathroom with a heat register under the window on the far wall?"

"Yeah, what is going on honey?"

I could feel the tension build. I was right on.

Her face grew concerned, "What happened, honey?"

"Well, this memory is of me standing in the bathroom in front of Jim and he made me... um... well... kiss his... thing."

Her face turned red, and an emotion flooded her face, which one, I was unsure. I could feel the heat emanating from her.

"If I got my hands on him right now, I would go to prison for life. I *knew* something happened; I just didn't know what it was."

Together we cried and I decided at that moment that I would not tell anyone else about this. I knew it broke her heart. She was the only person who knew about the molestation, and I planned to keep it that way.

The summer before my senior year my oldest sister got engaged to her girlfriend and asked me to be a bridesmaid. I was ecstatic. Expecting them to be as excited as I was, I told Dad and Jennifer. The pause on the other end of the phone made my heart drop.

"We will talk about this when you come back to Minnesota."

I knew I was in trouble.

I arrived home from the summer with my bio-mom and one of the first things we talked about was my sister's wedding. Due to the extreme evangelical views that they were convicted by, they basically forbade me to go to the wedding, but not in as many words. The back and forth was confusing and impossible. On one hand, I was finally being included on my biological mom's side of the family; on the other hand, I was potentially going against my 'faith' and allegiance to the very people who fed and housed me.

"You are old enough to make your own decisions, but just remember that if you don't stand up for Jesus on earth, He will not stand up for you in heaven."

The church taught us that homosexuality was an abomination. The eternal consequences were terrifying for me because I only knew that paradigm, that indoctrination. To drive the point home, Dad had the pastor and elders speak to me about the implications of participating in the wedding. They watched me as I wrote a letter to my sister explaining my decision to bow out of the wedding. It was a devastating blow to her, and to me. We didn't communicate for 13 years.

Two weeks into my senior year I was sitting in Senior Social Studies watching the am news like we did every day. The channel had a breaking news bulletin which most people ignored. Slowly the chatter in the room stopped and we all watched the screen, stunned. One plane went into a building. None of us realized what was happening for a couple of minutes... then we all realized that there were *actually* commercial jets plowing into the world trade center in New York City.

We watched in silence, jaws to the floor as the towers burned, as papers were plummeting from the windows, and eventually, as bodies plummeted. The coverage continued for a terrifying 15 minutes before there was news of another plane that crashed in a field, and then one that hit the Pentagon

People all over the country were trying to call their loved ones, only to hear on the other end of the line: "I'm sorry, this call cannot be completed at this time, please try again later". The cell towers and phone service carriers were overwhelmed, the bandwidth just wasn't broad enough for the entire country to be calling out at the same time.

I didn't know what this event meant, but I did know that the world would never be the same from this point on. The safety that we all took for granted had been shattered, and the feeling of floating above my body became more frequent, though I told no one.

ANNIKA ROSE

Secret's Out

Age 17

A couple of months later, our English teacher unknowingly started a mortifying chain of events in my life. One of our assignments was to pick a movie, watch it, and write a critique on it. During the discussion of our movies in class, one of the students began to share her critique. She chose a film which includes scenes of a dad flirting with, and sexually engaging with a teenage girl. She was defending how the story was beautiful... I honestly had no idea what her justification was for her assessment because my body started to react in a way I was unfamiliar with.

My blood began to grow hot, my face flushed, and suddenly, as if my face had a mind of its own, I hear myself say "That is disgusting!" It stunned the class, the teacher, and me.

As if it was a personal attack, the student shot back with "It's only a movie..."

I rebutted, she defended, ping pong insults across the room resulting in a full flashback of my abuse.

I yelled "Well, you obviously haven't experienced that then!!!"

I realized I had just outed myself and the molestation that I endured 11 years prior. I thought my face was on fire, my adrenaline was coursing through my veins like a freight train. I looked around the room realizing my mistake, ice filled my body, the world turned blurry.

Before I could catch up with my body, my desk was packed.

"Oh my God, I have to go, I have to go, I'm going, I have to go, I'm sorry, I have to go."

As I fled from the room, the students were left speechless.

I ran down the hall to my locker, opened it and started packing my bag to go home – forever – I was never coming back. Everyone knew and I just couldn't handle it. I didn't care about the repercussions, I just needed to escape.

About 3 minutes after I left the classroom, an acquaintance from my class came out,

"Are you okay? What happened??"

I dismissed her, "It happened when I was 5, it's over now, it's not a big deal".

My body continued to pack up my belongings as I watched from a few feet away. She tried to reassure me and invite me back to class, but that wasn't happening. I was comforted by her concern, but I was still hell-bent on escaping the situation.

Without much pause, the teacher came to my locker. "What happened to you?!"

"Nothing, it's nothing, I'm fine."

"I am a mandated reporter, and you have to tell me what happened."

When I wouldn't tell her, she grabbed my arm and dragged me to the guidance counselor's office.

The counselor shared a suite with the nurse's office, the school receptionist, and the social worker.

She flung door to the suite open, yelling "This girl has been molested; we need to talk to someone."

Faces from each of the rooms shifted their focus to me. I was mortified, terrified, and ashamed.

The social worker came out to see what the commotion was about and took me into a private room to talk.

"I am so sorry about all the attention you received back there." She knew the shame that was drowning me.

"Can you tell me what happened?"

I couldn't feel my arms. My face was clammy, and I held back the vomit that was fighting to escape my body.

"My step-dad molested me when I was 5, and when we were talking about movies in class, I accidentally blurted it out, and then the teacher dragged me down here saying I *had* to tell her what had happened."

Sobbing, I continued "Only my biological mom knows, please don't tell anyone, my dad will be so ashamed of me…"

"Dear, I am a mandated reporter. I must tell your parents and report it to the authorities. It's the law." She knew how impossible this all felt to me.

I protested, "It happened when I was 5, I don't live with him anymore, please don't tell anyone." My sobs turned to hopeless heaves, "Please don't tell my parents, they don't know, they will be so disappointed in me."

She thought about it, "Okay, well, your parents need to know, would you rather tell them?"

"Yes, if it has to happen." I gave in out of pure exhaustion.

"I do still need to contact the authorities."

Again, I argued, "It was 11 years ago in Chicago… what are they going to do? They are going to say, 'and… there are murders happening right now.'"

She conceded.

To add insult to injury, this was all happening on the Monday prior to the debut of the school musical *Bye Bye Birdie*. I was the mother in the production, and my husband, because of the small size of our town, was the school librarian.

Hurricane English teacher entered the suite again, this time with the principal and librarian in tow.

"This production cannot go on. It is highly inappropriate for a 17-year-old to play the *wife* of a full-grown adult *man*."

Students that were in the nurse's office were peeking around the corner, watching my life implode.

I begged them not to cancel the play, "Everyone in the town will know then! Please, I don't want people to know."

I floated above my body during my walk home. *How am I going to tell them?*

I floated to mom's home office, planting myself firmly on the guest bed that was to her back. My face was beet red and tear stained.

"Um, can we… um… talk?'. Terror filled my body.

She turned around, "Yeah."

I told her that Jim had molested me when I was 5, and as I cried, I told her how sorry I was.

She looked at me plainly, "I guess it happens to more people than I thought. I'm sorry."

There was no nurturing, no hugging, no reassurance. I begged her not to tell dad, though I knew that we would have to. She agreed temporarily.

A few days later we drove my little sister and brother to camp about 3 hours away, and on the ride back, mom prompted me to tell him.

"Um, Dad..."

"Yeah?" His eyes fixed firmly on the road, not ready for what I was about to tell him.

I told him what had happened. I had never heard so many swear words come out of his mouth. I thought he was mad at me, until he started to verbally contemplate revenge. He pulled the car over, got out and started pacing. I sat in the back of the van unsure of what he would do.

He got back in the car and we continued driving home. I could feel the anger that he was wearing like a cloak.

After that car ride, it wasn't really mentioned again. The school musical went on as scheduled and I finished my senior year. I graduated with honors and nervously anticipated the move north to college. A new start unencumbered by the trauma of my childhood.

A Whole New World

Age 18

The summer of 2002 was filled with packing my belongings. I was just barely 18 when I hopped in my little Geo Spectrum and began the three-hour journey to the university.

This was a fresh start, a beautiful adventure, complete freedom, and I was paralyzed with fear. Dad and Mom drove with me and helped me fit all my belongings in a 12-foot by 15-foot dorm room made for two. After everything was set up, we had a long, labored goodbye. I knew that this was my choice, but I felt abandoned all over again.

After the dust settled and it was quiet in the dorms, hot tears saturated my pillowcase, my body quietly heaved with sobs. I hadn't experienced social anxiety at this level ever before. I stayed in my upper bunk bed for over 48 hours, until I ran out of what food I had brought with me.

My roommate realized that I wasn't socializing and invited me to go down to the cafeteria with her and other floor mates. That was the first time (and one of the few times) that I ate there. I was overwhelmed by the 50-foot-long buffet, the different hot food stations, and the hundreds of students. The room turned into a blur and my thoughts raced. I heard the inner committee for the first time, all in different voices,

Are they watching me?

I'm so huge.

I can't do this.

Keep moving, there are people behind you.
You are in idiot.
Just leave.

Meal replacement shakes became a staple in my diet, supplemented only by salad and plates of carrots. I began to drop weight rapidly. I finally got the nerve to go to the campus gym mid-September. This space became my sanctuary, my safe place. The cardio room was dimly lit with neon recessed lighting creating the perfect environment for someone who didn't want to be seen. I was at the gym more often than anywhere else, clocking 3 to 4 hours per day.

During this same time, the groups and clubs on campus were in a frenzy to have students join their respective causes. It was not uncommon to be randomly invited to parties and events by complete strangers. One afternoon after class, a young woman stopped me and gave me a flyer inviting me to an event organized by Chi Alpha Christian Fellowship. I hesitantly showed up to the gathering, sipping water while standing near the wall, just observing. The over-eager students that ran the group descended on me and claimed me as their own.

Over a few weeks, I was able to relax, and Chi Alpha became my new comfort zone, second of course to the gym. I felt like I fit somewhere, like I belonged. I was wrapped up in the charismatic preaching, the dancing and crying in services, and the contemporary music. If I wasn't at a service, I was in a bible study, if not in a bible study, I was doing 'mission' work in the community. They were 'on fire' for Jesus and so was I.

I fared well in my classes even though I struggled to attend. I was relieved when Thanksgiving break rolled around because I was exhausted. I drove home and got a surprising reception. My family was happy to see me, but everyone was talking about my weight - both in front of me and behind my back.

Since I had left home 2 1/2 months earlier, I had lost 30 pounds. At 6 feet tall with a broad build, born of a midwestern fed linebacker of a dad, I had shrunk to a size 8. My hip bones were the hanger on which my pants hung. I was smaller than I had ever been. Hearing their concern irritated me - I had worked hard for these results and I was insulted that they were trying to bring me down. Besides, I was still overweight in my opinion.

Malnourishment and brain fog were my biggest competitor when it came to collegiate success. It was not uncommon for other students on my floor to find me passed out in the hallway, in the shower, or in the bathroom stalls. I am sure there were people who expressed concern over my weight, and I am positive that I disregarded them.

Over the holiday season, I went back home but was deeply uncomfortable. I went back to the dorms early. We still had church, even though there weren't many people on campus. I had gotten comfortable enough in the community that I began to sing in services and join the others at the local greasy spoon afterward.

One evening after worship, I was sitting in the first row of the auditorium chatting with a circle of friends when I saw a very large doc martin shoe kick my boot. I looked up to the very tall guy that owned said shoe. I know I had seen him around campus, but I had never had the desire to introduce myself. He was lanky with dirty blonde hair, cut in a predictable #2 on the sides, and 2 inches on top. He cut into the conversation as if I was the only person in the room,

"What are you doing?"

Somewhat irritated and offput, I looked around to my friends to gauge if I was the only one.

With blank faces all around, I answered, "Well, service is over, so we are going to the restaurant down the road for coffee and muffins." This was *not* an invite.

"Okay, where are we going?"

We? What is he talking about? What do I do?

Politely I said "Sure", and gave him the address.

He asked for my number in case he got lost and proceeded to pull out a permanent marker and wrote the 7 digits on his forearm.

Over the next week, he and I spent most of our time together. It seemed like everywhere I was, so was he. I was conflicted because I was not attracted to him and had a crush on another guy from the basketball team. It was uncanny how he was able to predict what I needed and wanted, always showing up to alleviate any things he perceived were my struggles. I was insecure about all of my attributes and his attention and charm were soothing my internal wounds.

The week before classes started again, it was my best friend's birthday. She reluctantly approved of his attendance at her birthday dinner, so we planned accordingly. He insisted on driving, which I thought was very gentlemanly of him. I was dressed in a black skirt and silver blouse, matched with 2-inch heels. He was still two inches taller than me, making me feel feminine and secure. He held the door of the suburban open and helped me into the truck. The chit chat on the way to the restaurant was pleasant, until it wasn't.

He took a wrong turn on the way there and became cold. I tried to lighten the mood because it was just a wrong turn, we could easily turn around.

He snapped at me, "I don't need your input, just let me drive."

I shut down until we got to the restaurant. I thought things would get better when we arrived at the venue. We got out of the truck and he began walking 3-4 feet ahead of me. I tried to catch up with him, but his stride was much longer than mine. He impatiently waited at the front door for me, sighing heavily when I got there.

When we walked in, I introduced him to all of my friends who immediately felt the tension. I picked at my quesadilla while he inhaled his plate of tacos. The checks came and Ian looked at me,

"How are you paying? Cash or card?"

I was kind of surprised but handed over my card. This was not my idea of a romantic date, not even successful really.

He was in a better mood on the drive back to the dorms, but I was still walking on eggshells. The walkway to my dorm was patched with ice. To play the hero and help me, Ian tried to pick me up. I had no idea what he was doing, so it was a failed attempt. He took it personally and the coldness came out again.

I hurried ahead to my group of friends, and he followed like a puppy to our dorm room. We packed 10 people into our little abode, Ian included. He and I sat on the futon, holding hands and eventually transitioned into cuddling. I was soaking it up, I had craved this feeling for *years*.

We ended up falling asleep until my obnoxiously loud alarm startled me awake. I opened my eyes, forgetting that he had fallen asleep with me. As the haze lifted, I could feel something behind me that indicated it was morning time for a man.

Mortified, I attempted to get off the futon without waking him. I slipped on the easiest outfit I owned, threw my hair in a ponytail, and left for class just as he was waking up. I just left him in my dorm wondering what had just happened. I never said a word. I panicked for the rest of the day and when I got back to my room, I called my dad.

Bawling, I blurted out "I slept with a guy last night!! I am so embarrassed and disappointed in myself! I'm so sorry!"

"Slow down honey, what happened?"

I told him the story and heard a chuckle on the other end of the phone.

"Oh honey, you need to make it clear whether you slept NEXT to someone or slept WITH someone."

"Oh God NO! I didn't sleep WITH him!"

We both laughed at the misunderstanding. Dad just said not to feel too bad and just make sure I am making healthy boundaries.

After that, I saw Ian one more time and then cut it off. I just couldn't reconcile the uneasiness I felt when I was around him, and I couldn't convince my friends that he was a good guy to keep around.

Valentine's day was just a few days after I cut Ian off. My roommate and I found ourselves single and lonely and went to hang out with a friend she had from high school. They were playing video games and drinking. We sat on the bunk beds and watched while our blood alcohol levels increased.

Once we were sufficiently loaded, she got a text from another friend, Jake. He was a few dorms down and had his friend from high school over. We excused ourselves from watching the video games to join them. We walked in to a haze of marijuana and bad beer. I knew I shouldn't be there but was drawn to Jake's friend.

Damon and I hopped onto the top bunk while Sarah and Jake occupied the lower bunk. After a couple minutes, I heard the other two making out. Damon and I giggled. He reached over and pulled me into him giving me my first kiss, then another, and another until we were in a full make out session.

Damon was high and started to go down on me. I didn't even know what it was until he started pulling my pants off and I protested strongly.

He said, "don't worry, we aren't going to have sex."

I was squirming and trying to get him to stop, I tried to keep my legs closed and he pried them apart assuring me that it would feel good. It did feel good, but I couldn't wait for him to finish. By the time he did, I had completely shut down.

He tried to get me to 'return the favor' but I began to cry and shamedly told him that I couldn't. I turned over and he held me, apologizing for going too far. We fell asleep and I woke up with a start at 9am realizing that I had a huge chorale concert at 11am. I ran back to my dorm, quickly donned the chorale dress, threw my hair in a ponytail, brushed my teeth, and took the freezing cold shortcut to the auditorium.

Damon and I became 'boyfriend and girlfriend' for about three weeks. He drove up to campus to surprise me the day before I left for a mission trip. I was shocked. I didn't like surprises, and this was a big one. After the shock wore off and I was able to finish packing for our trip, he and I talked, cuddled, and made out all night.

When I got back from my trip, he broke up with me over instant messenger. I felt my body turn to ice, overwhelmed with shame and shock. I called my biological mom in the middle of the night,

"He broke up with meeeeee, I really liked him mom."

She did her best to comfort me, knowing this was my first heartbreak.

My health began to decline rapidly. I started to see a counselor at the health services building who had me begin tracking my food intake. I remembered seeing her, but I didn't remember the content of our sessions. I couldn't remember much of anything.

Risky Business

Age 19

When the year ended, I decided not to move home for the summer. Instead, I moved in with my friend Veronica and her parents who were native to the small college town. I was preoccupied with a new love interest, Joe. He was 23, four years older than my 19-year-old self. We spent a lot of time out dancing and talking on the phone. One night at the beginning of the summer, he invited me over to his house which was about 45 miles away.

I arrived at 10:00pm to an empty house. I tried to get ahold of him, but his phone went to voicemail. His house was a small white single story ranch house in the middle of nowhere, surrounded by fir trees and a singular gravel road. After about 20 minutes, he called me and apologized, he was at a friend's house and would be home by 11:00. He said the house was open, and to make myself at home.

His house was indeed unlocked, and his two rottweilers met me at the door. They were so excited to have someone there. I couldn't figure out how to use his television, so I sat on the couch. 11:00 came and went, then 12:00am, my frustration began to mount with each passing minute. I fell asleep on his couch and was awoken by headlights coming up the driveway. He walked in, wasted. I looked at my watch... 3:00am.

He interrupted me right as I began to express my frustration,

"Come here beautiful."

I melted into his arms as he kissed me deeply. He locked me in the house, as we started heading toward the bedroom - I told him I didn't want to have sex. He assured me that he just wanted to lay down and watch tv instead of sitting in the living room. I acquiesced.

We passed the threshold and he pushed me onto the bed and thrust his clothed crotch in my face. I didn't even know what he wanted me to do. I kept getting more upset, then I crawled backwards to the head of the bed. He got in bed and apologized, then pinned me down and started working on my jeans. I was terrified. I left my body, praying that he would stop. He suddenly succumbed to the drunkenness and passed out.

I peeled my small body out from under his large frame, grabbed my purse as quickly as I could and fought the locked door before I was able to escape to my car. I got about a half hour away before I was overtaken by a full panic attack. I called Veronica.

"What did you expect?", she said with an air of irritation and disinterest.

I arrived home at 5:00am, fell into my bed and cried.

The next day, Joe called me and asked if everything was okay. I was floored. "NO, everything *isn't* okay!"

He was shocked, "What do you mean? I thought we had a good time, sorry for falling asleep…" He had no memory of anything that happened. He remembered driving in the driveway and waking up alone.

I told him what had happened and told him that I didn't want to talk to him again.

I spent the summer of 2003 going to the beach, dancing, and hanging out with different groups of friends. Veronica and her brother were known for being amazing sports stars in town, and we often spent time at the men's frat house. At the end of the summer, they had their big back to school party. Of course we went. I normally never drank, but Veronica assured me that we had a designated driver, so I agreed to one drink, made by her brother – I figured that was a safe bet.

The drink he made me was very strong. I remember taking a few sips and sitting on the couch. There are flashes of memory… dancing in the living room… sitting on the stairs… talking to her brother in one of the upstairs rooms… and waking up with my shirt pulled up and my pants unbuttoned next to him in his bed at 3am.

Confused, I wandered around and quickly realized that the party was over, and my designated driver had left. I was terrified and livid. I got one of my trusted friends out of his room and demanded that he take me home.

Still in a fog, I tried to navigate the stairs and getting into bed. I woke up the next morning just as angry as when I passed out. I quickly figured out that I had been roofied. I reamed Veronica out. I couldn't understand why they would leave me there. She said I was super obnoxious and wanted to stay. I didn't know what to think.

Word got out that I was angry and I began to receive texts from the various housemates,

"I wouldn't go to the cops if I were you."

"You asked for it."

"How are you going to prove anything?"

"If you report us, you will get a minor and get kicked out of college."

I was shamed into silence.

Two weeks later, I stood in my room with a lethal dose of opiates in my left hand and a glass of water in the right when my phone rang. A friend from church had a feeling she should call, and I admitted that I just couldn't do it anymore. She rushed to the house, pried the pills from my hand and took me to the campus counselor.

Things got tense living with Veronica, but I spent most of my time at school, at the gym, work, church, or at other friend's houses. I continued to lose weight, even though I was emaciated.

ANNIKA ROSE

Rekindled

Age 19

Ian, the guy that I dated briefly a year prior, started to call me again early in the fall semester of 2003. He was asking for prayer and scripture to help him with depression and suicidality. He knew that my faith was super important, that I had dealt with mental health issues, and that I was an empath. He and I had been talking more, he was writing me poetry, and really charming me.

On December 10, 2003, a friend and I made an impulsive decision to drive 3 hours in a blizzard to see her boyfriend and Ian. We stayed at Ian's parent's home, where he lived. We played pool and watched movies, and when it was time for bed, I followed Ian to his bedroom.

We settled into bed, talking about different things when he looked at me seriously,

"Do you want to be together again?"

The butterflies in my stomach swelled. "Do you??"

He kissed me deeply and pulled me close whispering, "You have to promise that our last breakup will never happen again."

The familiar cold feeling flooded my veins… *does he own me now?* I ignored the feeling and fell asleep, warm in his arms.

We began seeing each other more often. By Christmas I met his family and by New Years, we were in love. I spent New Year's Eve at his parent's house because we hosted a party.

Before his friends showed up, we were sitting on the couch and I noticed he was quiet. In an effort to lift the energy I smiled and turned to him,

"I'm really excited to meet your friends! Do you think they'll like me?"

He looked disgusted, "Not with you looking like that..."

"What do you mean..."

He walked away in the middle of my sentence.

I was mortified, and angry. I changed clothes, not knowing what was so bad about how I looked, but dropping the subject because we didn't have enough time for a fight. I was determined to be a gracious hostess and to live up to what Ian and his friends would find valuable.

His friends showed up, and so did Wendy, his prior girlfriend. Ian wrapped his arm around my waist and introduced me with hearts in his eyes. *Wait, I guess we are okay now?*

I started to drink - a lot. I still wasn't eating, but I was taking pulls from a Captain Morgan bottle like it was water. Wendy and I were playing pool when I leaned into her to tell her a secret,

"You knowww what?? I just want you to know, that I have always been jealous of you. You are so beautiful, and he obviously liked you so much and I'm not as pretty or small as you, ya knowww?"

She put her hand on my back, "Don't worry, he obviously picked you over me, and you are gorrrrrgeous."

I didn't realize at the time that he was destroying her while he groomed me.

Shortly after the clock turned midnight and 2004 arrived, I laid on the cool tile of his bathroom in the fetal position. I noticed the long pauses between the beats of my heart. I started to pray "I'm so sorry that this is how I am going to meet You God." Ian came in, tried to wake me up, then he picked me up from the floor and placed me on his bed. He yelled at his friends to get a pan so I could throw up and then started urging me to get rid of the alcohol if I could.

"Should we call 911" one of his friends said panicked.

Ian and the rest of the guys echoed the same sentiment: "We will all get minors!"

I ended up throwing up, then fell asleep.

Two short months later, Ian took me to dinner and a movie for Valentine's Day. I wore my roommate's size 8 little black dress, curled my hair, and strapped on some heels. After the movie, he took me on a tour of his

60

hometown. Once we got to his childhood church, we parked the car and started talking. About 5 minutes in, he turned to me, took my hand in his, and stuttered,

"What do, I mean, how do you feel about, well, will you marry me?"

I remember looking at him doe-eyed and realizing that I had never rehearsed what to say for an engagement, so I stuttered "I do, um, I accept, uh YES!!!"

It didn't occur to me that we had only been dating for 2 months and that it was a spontaneous idea on his part. He didn't have a ring, but I had just gotten my student loan money, so we went to pick out the ring. He assured me he would pay me back for the ring and that he was so proud to be engaged to me.

He knew my position on pre-marital sex, but a couple of nights later, while making out, he tried to persuade me to try "it" just to see if we were a good fit. I protested, reminding him that I really wanted to wait for marriage. We went back and forth for a while between kisses and advances. He was already on top of me and I finally silently conceded as he entered me. When he had finished, he left to clean up while I silently sobbed. I felt so gross, like I was disappointing God, like I was a hypocrite, like I was a dirty girl all over again.

As we moved forward in our relationship, his coercion became more intense. "It's natural", "Don't you love me?", "We've done it once, why would it matter now?" After a while, I caught him looking at porn and I was devastated. He said it was my fault because I wouldn't let him have sex with me. Our sex got more violent and verbally abusive. I suffered in near silence - though I wrote about it. I cried every time.

I was attempting to finish the spring semester despite my rapidly failing health. In March 2004, I got bad cramps and couldn't move without passing out. My roommate's mom took me to the hospital where they pumped me full of fluids and sent me home with pain meds. My depression increased and I began to fail my classes. In retrospect I realize that I was literally dying.

The final straw was in April. I was walking from the music department to my car when I got lightheaded. I sat on the entryway stairs and began to shake and sweat profusely. I texted a friend to come get me because I knew something was very wrong. Right after that text, I passed out at the bottom of the stairs. Students literally stepped over my body to get to where they were going. I vaguely remember one girl asking if I was okay. I don't remember what I mumbled to her, but she left.

My friend arrived and helped me off the floor. I knew I was going to be sick, so she walked me to the bathroom. I sat on the toilet, doubled over, and my body let go of everything. I started shaking uncontrollably, going in and out of consciousness. She handed me my phone.

"What is going on?" My mom's voice came through the speaker.

"Mom, I'm sick, I don't know what's…" I trailed off.

Shortly after that, EMTs were hauling me out of the bathroom and carting me into the ambulance where they took my vitals.

"Oh my Lord, look at her blood pressure, she should be dead right now."

I don't remember being in the hospital, I just remember that I was lonely because none of my people were with me.

Again, I was sent home with opiates to handle the period pain that I was enduring. Two days later, I was holding the pills in my left hand, and a glass of water in the right when Veronica came in and pried the meds out of my hand.

I moved home a week later at the request of Ian and our parents. By the end of April, I had come down with a terrible case of MONO. All I could do was sleep on a mattress in my mom's home office, cry, and eat scrambled eggs. Ian stayed with me every night, quietly having sex with my worn-out body so as not to wake my mom who was sleeping in the next room. During the day, at the behest of my parents, he worked hard to convince me to go to treatment for my eating disorder. I was terrified of gaining weight, and I asked him if he would still love me if I got fat. He hesitated for a full day. The next day, he gave me a note, "I will love you no matter what weight you are."

I agreed to go to treatment.

Unwritten Rules

Ages 20-21

Ian's parents lived near the hospital, so I moved into their house temporarily while I went into partial inpatient eating disorder treatment in May 2004. I spent 7:00am to 7:00pm at the hospital Monday through Friday attending therapy, groups, dietician appointments, and eating meals and snacks under clinical supervision. This phase normally lasts 4-6 weeks with a step down to 3-4 days per week for 4-6 weeks, and then outpatient from then on.

After 4 weeks of treatment, Ian became restless and noted the weight gain that I was experiencing as a result of eating more than the pre-treatment regimen of 800 calories per day. He began to drop hints that his parents were wanting me to find my own place and that we can't afford an apartment if I am in treatment.

"I'm so excited to marry you, baby. Can we agree to save every penny and not to spend a dime? As a matter of fact, let's use that as a motto in order to prepare for the wedding."

Being the people pleaser I was, and under the threat of running out of money and a place to live, I decided to end treatment and start the next chapter of my life.

I moved back home to live with my newly separated dad in his new townhome. I applied for cosmetology school and started classes in August of 2004. I found my place in the world. I took to the skills almost immediately and became a well sought-after student for the community members that came in for services.

Ian supported my schooling and gave me the love that I craved. He made my lunches for me and brought them to the college; he went as far as to sell his bass amp so I was able to go to the International Beauty Show in Chicago.

The sweetness didn't stop there. His mom was in love with me. She and I spent most weekends together going store to store, trying on clothes and loading bags upon bags into the back of her Mercedes. All the while, planning the wedding that was to take place in the summer of 2006.

I had never had the feeling of security in this way. I was swept off my feet by the perception of safety and unconditional love. I felt seen and heard, secure and hopeful.

Around the holidays in 2004, Ian began to point out the 'toxicity' of my family. He had an uncanny ability of finding one instance of my family hurting my feelings and from that, painting a broad picture of the vitriol that my family had toward me. The contrast between what he and his family did for me against the picture he painted of my family created an unbearable dissonance.

At first, I fought the notion that my family was bad. Sure, my bio-mom gave me to my dad, my step-mom and dad were getting a divorce, my siblings were acting out on their teenage angst, and none of my parents were paying for my schooling, but that was normal right? I argued with him, telling him how my family did the best that they could with what they had, just like everyone in this world.

Each argument I made triggered a 4-hour monologue where he assured me of his love and support. He professed that he had my best interest at heart, that it was he and I against the world. Point after point, assurance after assurance, day after day, monologue after monologue blurring my mind until I became convinced that my family was unhealthy and causing me to go backward, away from him. After all, didn't I love him?

I steadily gained weight after treatment, as one does. My energy increased and my mood followed. I graduated in August of 2005 and was immediately hired as a makeup artist for a store in the mall. I moved to my first apartment, a studio. It was only 450 square feet, but it was mine. Ian spent most of his time at my place even though he lived only 5 minutes away in his parent's house.

The security I felt from earning my own money, using my talents, and directing my own life was intoxicating. It would have been nice to have my apartment alone every now and then, but I didn't want to take Ian's love for granted, and I really looked forward to the snuggling and safety I felt at night.

That security was solid until I woke up one night to him lightly pinching my lower stomach fat, measuring it. I felt the blood in my veins turn to ice. I didn't give any indication that I was awake, afraid to start a fight and endure the subsequent monologue. I gave a deep sigh and stretched, turning on to my stomach and falling asleep again.

The measurements began to be a regular thing while I was 'sleeping', and soon there was a scale in 'our' apartment. Conversations began to revolve around growing old together, what that would look like, and the need to be healthy enough to fulfill all 'our' dreams. As a gift, Ian gave me a workout DVD that came with a meal plan touting the newest fad, 'The Mediterranean Diet". He began doing the shopping and meal planning so I could focus on working and getting 'stronger'.

In October of 2005, he and I drove 10 hours south to visit my bio-mom. He was his usual charming self, bringing her flowers and thanking her for her hospitality. Everything was going smoothly, and I was impressed at his gracious behavior.

A couple of nights in, we were making out in my room, and he cupped the back of my head with his hand and began to apply pressure. I recoiled,

"I don't want to do that babe, I'm sorry."

He let up pressure and kissed me. "It's okay baby, I understand."

About 5 minutes later, he did it again, this time with more strength. I tried to pull back, but he whispered,

"Don't worry, I'm helping you heal from your step-dad".

A tear escaped out the side of my right eye as he pressed himself into my mouth. I escaped mentally while he used my body. When he was relieved, he pulled me close,

"You did so well baby, I'm so proud of you. It will get easier and easier."

I excused myself to go clean up, closed the bathroom door behind me, and began to cry, hyperventilating and choking on my tears.

My mom could hear me and called me into her bedroom where she was watching tv. I crawled into bed with her in the fetal position and sobbed uncontrollably. I explained what had happened and just as I was finishing the story, Ian walked down the hall, leaning against the door frame,

"What's going on? Are you okay, baby?", as if nothing had happened.

I sat up in the bed, "Yeah, I just missed mom and am glad to be here."

We went back to bed, never mentioning the situation again.

Preparations

Age 21

In November, we really started to plan for the wedding, including learning to be a Godly husband and wife. We went through mandatory marriage counseling with the officiant at the church. Pastor Brian was sincere and genuine.

We had one-on-one counseling with him as part of the pre-marriage counseling process. During one of my sessions, he got serious for a minute,

"Hailey, I can't tell you what to do, but I do not feel that Ian is a good man for you. I don't believe your marriage would be as successful as it could be. Of course, it is ultimately your decision, but I wouldn't be doing you a service if I didn't tell you."

I never mentioned that to Ian, fearing if I had that we would have to change churches.

At the same time, the divorce between my dad and step-mom was final and my dad was convinced that a lack of respect was the culprit in his marriage. The weekend before Thanksgiving, the three of us attended a *Love and Respect* conference at our church which was put on by author Dr. Emerson Eggerichs. The premise was that God created men to desire respect, and women to desire love, and that the only way to have a successful marriage was for wives to respect their husbands and husbands to love their wives.

I took notes furiously, filling page after page with how to respect Ian and be a 'good Christian wife'. The principle was an eye opener for me, a catalyst for deep guilt and a renewed commitment to loving Ian in the way that he needed.

There was a 10-minute segment of the conference which focused on the idea that women can respect their husband by maintaining a good appearance. This seemed to be the only thing Ian took from the whole experience.

After the weekend, Ian began to tell me that he felt disrespected by my body. The monologues became nightly, echoing the same sentiment.

"We aren't even married yet and you've let yourself go."

He alluded to the fact that if I didn't lose weight, he wouldn't marry me. "This isn't what I signed up for."

During each 'conversation', I would cautiously remind him of the note he gave me before treatment in which he told me he'd love me at every weight.

He would reply coldly, "You didn't tell me it would be this much."

Despite my best efforts, he wore me down. In order to get back to the weight that he met me at, I had to lose 60 pounds before the wedding, which was six months away. I was so eager to respect him, especially since my family was distant from me at this point. His parents were supportive of our new focus on healthy living, doing whatever they could to support us.

He suggested that our new motto should be "Eat less, work out more", in addition to the existing motto, "Save every penny and don't spend a dime."

He started to monitor my food and weight and praised me for my workouts.

The more I lost, the happier he became. "Baby, I just love you so much, and I can't fathom living without you. The only way to live long together is to be healthy by eating less and working out more. You've got this beautiful."

The weight began to fall off, but it was okay, it was just because I was eating healthy and working out – it wasn't my eating disorder. Also, if it was my eating disorder, his family wouldn't approve, right?

By May of 2006, my pants were falling off and my wedding dress was fitted to my new slim figure. The RSVPs had been returned, the seating chart was set, and the music chosen. A week before the wedding, I decided to have a conversation with Ian as a final get out of jail free card, should he need it.

"So, I need to make sure that you know that I want kids and travel more than anything in the world. Those are my deal breakers. If you don't want them, that is totally fine, just tell me now and we can walk away, no hurt feelings."

Although taken aback, he didn't miss a beat, "Baby, of course I want those things. I can't think of anything more beautiful than making children that are just ours and seeing the world with you. I love you more than anything, we are in this together."

ANNIKA ROSE

The Big Day

Age 21

With the assurance of children and travel that Ian gave me, I eagerly went into the pre-wedding week. By this time, I was the assistant manager of my salon, had lost 60 pounds and was looking forward to a beautiful life with him - everything seemed perfect.

The night before the wedding, all my bridesmaids slept over at my apartment with me. I was excitedly nervous and as much as I tried, I couldn't fall asleep. Finally, my best friend from high school came into my bed and soothed my nerves by running her fingers through my hair as I fell asleep.

The alarm blared at 6:00 am, waking me from my last night of singlehood. We packed up and got to the salon by 7:00 with my hair being curled and pinned by 7:30. We were all aware of the time crunch, as we had to be to the church by 9:00 am for the 11:00 am wedding.

At 9:15 my vehicle, driven by a bridesmaid, sped into the parking lot. I was just finishing my makeup in the passenger side visor mirror when my mom ushered me out of the vehicle and into the bridal suite.

The room was beautiful, fitted with a private dressing area behind an oriental room divider, a long table with refreshments, and a photo area with a full-length mirror.

First things first, I had to get out of my sweats, wrangle myself into the corset, and step into my dress. It was a gorgeous tailored a-line white satin and lace gown covered with looping pearls cascading down the bodice. I stood in front of the mirror as my mom zipped it up around my whittled frame. A beautifully beaded veil was attached to my professionally coiffed crown of blonde curls, completing the look.

The photographer positioned me in various areas to memorialize the wedding preparations. As I stood in front of the full-length mirror, my stepmom was posed behind me, her face proud and nostalgic. After a few photos, she took a serious posture and turned me around to face her,

"You know, you don't have to do this. You can back out right now if you want."

What? No way! There were people from all over coming to celebrate this day!

Cooly, I responded, "No, I do not need to back out."

I couldn't help the voices in the back of my head, worrying about what Ian would think of my body. I wanted more than anything to make him proud, to assure him that he was making the right decision. Only time would tell what his reaction would be.

The wedding coordinator arranged a 'first look' where Ian stood with his back to me as I walked up to him. When instructed to do so, he slowly turned, his face morphing from curiosity to admiration and then surprise. He looked star struck and feigned tears of happiness. Relief washed over me; my work had paid off, he was happy.

We took group pictures as we prepared for the ceremony. While lined up on the stairs with our family and friends, the photographer yelled "Say cheese!".

Through a forced smile, Ian wrapped his arm around my waist whispering "Suck in, these photos are forever."

Determined to enjoy my day, I pushed aside his comment, straightened my back, and smiled genuinely at the camera lens.

It was time. I began to walk up to the back of the church to meet my dad. Somewhere between the front of the church and the foyer, one of my aunts pulled me aside,

"You know you can just walk away right now, right? If this doesn't feel right, we support you in cancelling the wedding."

Why is everyone so dead set on me backing out?!

Exasperated and irritated, I brushed her off, "No, I am fine, this is really what I want."

She faded away as I found my dad. He was standing tall, stoic, his nerves rivaled mine in that moment. I looped my right arm through his left.

"Whelp, I guess this is it, huh?" I looked up at him looking for reassurance.

"Yep, here we go." He took the first step and I followed.

We walked down the aisle focusing on our feet, *don't trip, don't trip, more than anything… don't trip.* I briefly noted how numb I felt. Wasn't I supposed to feel elated, royal, adored? I just felt… nothing.

I heard the complementary whispers from the crowd and watched Ian don his public, picture taking smile. We approached the front, where I was supposed to leave my dad, where my life would change forever, where I was no longer protected. I physically felt the emotional separation as my dad let my arm go.

Suddenly, I felt unsafe, unprotected, and vulnerable. This was truly *it.*

Ian took my hand and led me up the stairs to stand in front of the officiant. Shaking with anticipation, I looked into Ian's eyes searching for comfort and reassurance. He looked so happy, so proud. The officiant's words were blurred, fuzzy around the edges. My brain was not processing what he was saying. Finally, it came time to exchange our vows. Everything came into focus; the focus was on me. *Repeat exactly as he says, don't mess it up.*

Time skipped again and I found myself at the altar while a familiar woman sang a song that I apparently had picked out. She sang about a couple who love each other in the worst times, through grey hair and wrinkles, gain and loss, of an unending love. I squeezed Ian's hand,

"This is us baby. We did it."

His hand was limp and his body cold, "No it's not."

I was shocked, embarrassed. Tears streamed down my face. *Why can't I be good enough?*

We turned toward the crowd and were announced to our friends and family as husband and wife. We began the walk to the back of the church. Waiting for us was a table with the marriage certificate and two pens. I stared at it for a minute, I didn't remember ever getting the certificate, let alone that we had to sign it. Everything felt foreign.

I leaned down to sign the paper and noticed that my signature did not look like mine. I chalked it up to adrenaline and nervous shakes. When I set the pen down, I felt like the jail doors slammed – I was no longer my own, I was owned.

While our guests went to the reception hall, Ian and I were brought to a separate room where our meal was laid out for us. We had roasted chicken with garlic green beans and baby red potatoes. I began to eat, noticing the energy shifting, I looked up at him as he started in,

"Are you watching your calories? If you eat all this, can you afford to have wedding cake?"

I got irritated, "Our wedding day should be a day to just have fun."

He started the "Slippery slope" speech. I prayed that it would end before we had to go down to the reception to greet our guests.

He finished his speech and the coordinator escorted us to the reception hall where our guests were eating their entrees. We walked table to table, mingling with our friends and family, thanking them for celebrating with us, receiving their love and support. This was the best part of the wedding, by far.

Soon, the glass clinking started, signaling that it was time for Ian and I to kiss in front of everyone. We rose from the head table and Ian dipped me backward while we kissed. My dress got caught on the chair and we stumbled. I laughed because it was a fluke, and everyone was in light spirits. Ian did not take it so lightly. He was angry. I gave him passes because I knew that he was stressed out.

The time to cut the cake had arrived. My anxiety spiked, but at this point, I was a professional at hiding it. Behind a beautiful smile, I accepted that I was unable to eat the cake due to the lunch I had and the munching I had done just prior to the wedding.

We took the ornate cake knife in our hands and cut the first piece. We fed each other the cake, rather, Ian smeared mine on my lips and I fed him. Once the photos were done, I spit out what small amount of cake had made it to my mouth – it tasted *so* good, while it lasted.

We invited everyone to the in-law's house for the after party and gift opening. Jennifer had gifted me a beautiful pink linen party dress from Filene's Basement. I went into Ian's parent's bedroom to change out of my gown and into the party dress.

Ian unzipped the gown for me and let it pool at my ankles. We had a passionate kiss, our first in private as a married couple. As I was changing, he bent me over the bed.

"Babe, not now, we have to get out there, everyone is waiting. We can play at the hotel later."

He didn't listen and had his way with my body. I convinced myself that I liked it, after all, I was his now spiritually and physically.

I changed into my party dress. Ian whispered to me as we walked to the living room,

"Please suck in, you look like you have a spare tire in that dress."

ANNIKA ROSE

The First Night

Age 21

After the party, we arrived at the hotel where we would spend the night before flying to Hawaii. This was our first night as a married couple, and we were exhausted.

We walked into the double queen room around 7:00pm to find that my mom and sister had been there already. On the bathroom vanity sat a basket filled with lingerie, champagne, candies, and other goodies for us to enjoy on our first night.

Excitedly I grabbed the white lace bralette and thong and disappeared into the bathroom. My mind raced.

Now that I'm not going to resist, it's going to be beautiful and loving.

Lip-gloss, no, he doesn't like the stickiness, lip stain, yes.

I hope I look sexy enough for him, I want him to want me, not just take me.

Powder on my face, down my neck, and into my cleavage.

We are finally going to be having sex in the confines of marriage, no more guilt!

Deodorant and Sweet Pea body spray.

This is it, God please let me turn him on.

I semi-confidently emerged from the bathroom, striking a pose for my new husband to enjoy, only to find him stomach down, laying across the hotel bed diagonally, sleeping.

I set my high hopes aside, slipping into bed, snuggling up to his sleeping body, quickly falling asleep as well.

We woke up at about 3:00am. He lovingly pulled me in close, whispering how much he loved me, slowly pulling my lingerie down. He made love to me, safe love, pleasurable love, married love. Satisfied, we both drifted to sleep before we had to leave for the airport.

The morning alarm came quickly. I woke up like a kid on Christmas morning. I had never flown over the ocean. In my mind, palm trees danced, and hula dancers swayed. Ian isn't a morning person, but I didn't pay him any mind, I was too excited.

Almost Paradise

Age 21

We arrived at the airport two hours early knowing it would take a long time to get through the multi-layer checks and scans. Once through security, we took a collective sigh of relief and found our gate.

I could tell that Ian's energy was becoming more withdrawn and frantic, something to pay attention to but not yet address as we were in public.

We couldn't board fast enough. My anticipation was almost too big for my body to hold. My enthusiasm may have been, in part, an appeal to Ian to also get into a positive headspace, although unsuccessful. Nevertheless, I was taking in each moment so I wouldn't forget anything.

We boarded the plane and took our seat in the first row of coach class. He is 6'4" and I am 6'0". Aside from the exit row, the first row was the only area where our knees wouldn't jet into someone else's back.

Ian's hands were shaking. *What? He's afraid of flying??* I took his hand in mine and told him it would be okay. He ignored me. I pulled the "Sky Mall" magazine from the pocket ahead of us and convinced him to leaf through, page by page, choosing the things that we wanted to buy for our fictitious palatial mansion. Full body massage chair, Olympic swimming lane, infinity edge pool, 11-in-1 blender with speaker, and on and on.

The flight from Minneapolis to Hawaii was *loooooong*. Five hours to our layover in Portland, and then another eight to Honolulu.

I had always imagined that our first meal in Hawaii would be exotic and romantic, donning leis and drinking Mai tais. To my dismay, it ended up being a meal from Burger King in the Honolulu airport. Another grilled chicken sandwich with diet coke.

I was exhausted and getting irritable at Ian's incessant nagging and complaining. I was not surprised that Ian would have an issue with what we were doing, but I needed to eat, and thus ignored him.

As we began to eat our 'American fare', there were kids goofing around and whining to their mom nearby. Most people would have ignored them, or even shot the mom a sympathetic smile. Not Ian. He grew increasingly angry, looked at me with daggers in his eyes,

"We are not having kids, and there will be no more travelling".

I joked with him to see if he was serious, "You don't mean that, you are just tired."

"Did you hear what I said?"

I retreated into myself; he was serious.

My heart was shattered, the shackles tightened. Just a week ago he promised these two things to me. He lied to me, he trapped me, and I couldn't do anything to escape. In our religion, divorce was not an option, and I was committed to being a godly Christian wife, no matter the circumstance. For better or worse, right?

I offered no comfort on our final flight to the beautiful island of Kauai. I was over trying to make him feel better. It wasn't long before I completely forgot that he was pouting, the awareness erased by the beautiful women waiting at the bottom of the jetway, eager to put leis around our necks and usher us into luxury.

Our rental car was a red Ford Mustang convertible. Sexy car for a sexy couple. I couldn't wait to drive it. Ian drove us to the hotel where we would spend the next 8 days. The ocean front property was surrounded by palm trees and native greenery. Our room was, well, a room.

Once settled in, we walked down to the beach. Waves lapped on the sand, I took a deep breath of sea breeze and wrapped my arms around his waist.

"I'm so grateful for you baby. Thank you for marrying me."

He accepted the affection, "I'm sorry for being so harsh today, it was just a really hard trip for me."

I understood, "Let's just move forward and enjoy our time here."

As always, Ian reminded me of our mottos, *eat less and work out more,* and *save every penny and don't spend a dime.* I knew that the consequence for not working out 2 hours per day and counting my calories was a 4-hour word salad of circular reasoning meant to wear me down and push me into submission. When I briefly objected, using my back pain as a possible out, he came back with,

"There are always special occasions, if we slipped every time, we would never be doing what we are supposed to. To be honest, you said you were going to lose more weight before the wedding, we can't really afford to indulge right now. After all, the goal is to live a long healthy life together. Don't you want that?"

At this point, my memory becomes intermittent, however, there was one woman that made a lasting impression.

We took an early morning walk down the road to a small outdoor market where we perused different local artisan creations. A small unassuming sarong kiosk lured me with its bright colors and flowing fabrics. A stout and deeply tan woman with long white hair welcomed us. She was no taller than my shoulder. Her energy was grounded, powerful, nurturing. I found safety in her words; her conversation was a balm to my overextended nervous system.

"Are you guys here for your honeymoon?!" She asked.

I wrapped my arms around Ian's waist, "Mhmm."

He shrunk back as I continued to entertain her story.

"How long have you lived in Hawaii? I'm from Minnesota, so this is paradise."

"I have lived here for 20 years – the land healed me." Her eyes glowed with peace.

I was intrigued and Ian excused himself from the conversation. "What do you mean *it healed you?*"

She went on to explain that she was diagnosed with stage 4 ovarian cancer and was given 6 months to live, so she moved to Hawaii. Six months came and went, all the while feeling stronger and healthier. She went in for a new scan… to her surprise, and the surprise of everyone involved, there was no cancer, it was gone. No one knows how it happened, but she swears it was the magic of the islands.

I was aghast. Miracles still happen, things *do* get better.

From the market, we hopped into the mustang and drove to the small airport on the island. We were scheduled for a helicopter ride around the perimeter of the island. Excitedly, we walked into the small office where we would sign in and watch a quick video on what to expect.

Part of signing in was weighing in. They needed to evenly distribute the weight throughout the cabin. I turned ice cold; the blood ran from my head to my feet in a single moment. I hadn't weighed myself since I got to the hotel and it was a relief not to have Ian on my back about my weight.

Please weigh 193, please weigh 193.

I closed my eyes and stepped on the scale. When I slowly opened my eyes a large "203" showed up on the screen. I knew I was in trouble. I didn't dare look at Ian because I could already feel his anger.

"What the fuck" he hissed under his breath.

Attempting to delay the berating I said, "Can we please wait to have this conversation?"

The clerk at the counter was unsure of what to do or say. We finished checking in and sat down for the 5-minute presentation on the risks of taking a helicopter ride.

As if he was going to explode if he didn't speak up, he whispered, "Have you been lying to me about your calories?"

"No, of course not. Flying and PMS made me gain water weight. I promise it will come off."

"It better."

From then on, he walked either in front of me or behind me, ashamed to be seen with me. He begrudgingly had sex with me once or twice. He constantly asked about my calories, pinched my fat, told me I would be embarrassing both of us if I showed my body in a bathing suit. I continued to try to stay positive, flirt with him, please him, etc. Nothing worked.

There were brief moments when he was kind and romantic, but only when people were watching.

By the last day of our honeymoon, I had lost all hope that I would be able to please my new husband. I remember sitting in the airport with tears leaking from my eyes, I felt like the worst wife ever.

A New Normal

Age 21-22

Disclaimer: My memory is very spotty between ages 22 and 25. I have done my best to recall the events, but this is not, by any means, a complete view of what happened during that timeframe.

The flight home did not elicit the anticipatory mood I had hoped to feel. We were beginning our life together and I already felt like I had to play catch up. I felt defeated, discouraged, and down. I resigned to his mood and did whatever I could to avoid aggravating him.

By the time the plane landed, I had pulled myself together and put on the happy enamored persona that was needed to survive. We excitedly told his parents all about the trip and thanked them for covering it. They drove us to the apartment where we found the pile of wedding gifts in the center of the living room. I was so grateful for the love that our family and friends showered us with.

One of the gifts was a laser cut Waterford crystal serving bowl that a dear family friend had given us. I planned on putting decorative lemons in it and centering it on our dining room table to create a fresh and open feeling in our small space. For some reason this bothered Ian. After a few weeks of settling in, I couldn't find the bowl, and I never saw it again.

So much happened in our first month of marriage. Ian's parents bought a brand-new car for me so I had a reliable form of transportation and I was promoted to manager at one of the salons that my Franchisee owned. I found safety behind the salon chair, and I was truly passionate about growing my staff and my salon. I was working 40-50 hours per week and the success of the salon increased in proportion to the amount of time I was there. The stress was mounting, and my severely restricted diet affected both my ability to advocate for myself and to make boundaries. Despite my inner struggle, Ian and I continued to push forward.

Due to my weight at the Hawaiian helicopter ride, I sat through multiple 4-hour monologues about being healthy and living long lives together and how my weight could cause me to die early. He asserted that he had done his research about my body type and determined that my ideal weight was 193lbs to 197lbs. This seemed feasible as I only had to lose 4 pounds to be in that range. His rants wore me down and by the end I was exhausted and complied just so I could go to bed.

Three months after the wedding I had surgery to relieve the excruciating pain that my endometriosis caused. During the surgery, they cut through my abdominal wall causing swelling and requiring a week or two of reduced weight bearing ability. Luckily, we were able to go up to his parent's lake home so I could focus on healing.

While we were loading the car to go, Ian asked me to carry out a box that was roughly 20 pounds. My protest fell on deaf ears. I stepped out of the door and collapsed against the wall overcome with dizziness and a full body sweat. I simply was not strong enough.

I heard the hallway door open and was embarrassed to see that it was my neighbor. He saw me and asked me in a hushed tone,

"Are you okay? Is he hurting you?"

"Oh my gosh, *no* he's not. I just had surgery and thought I was invincible, thanks for checking in though!"

He hesitantly said "Okay, just wanted to make sure..." then he walked away.

I don't think he believed me.

Losing Control

Ages 22-25

During our marriage, Ian went through multiple colleges. He got very excited about a career path, convinced everyone around him that it was the greatest idea, and then pushed forward in that new trajectory. Any time that I brought up concerns that I was the only one bringing in substantial income, he reminded me that our goal was for him to make enough money for me to eventually go back to school. I was also painfully aware that we needed to pay his parents back for how they had helped me financially. I was convinced that as a 'team' we were going to both be able to stay healthy, save money, and handle our financial commitments.

Ian took the reins in our finances because he didn't trust that I was being honest with "saving every penny and not spending a dime". I handed all my tips into him when I came home from work, trusting that he was depositing them into our checking account.

I enjoyed doing small things to show him that I cared. On a summer day, I drove to the college while he was in class to clean his truck and leave a love note on his seat. I unlocked the Tahoe and noticed a couple of things that caught me off guard. First was a small girly keychain on the floor behind his driver's seat. I thought maybe it was from before we got together? Second, there were fast food bags littering the back seat – he was spending my tips on fast food. I went home with the love note in my pocket.

When he arrived home, I asked him about the keychain and fast-food bags. He accused me of not trusting him while he was working to make a better life for us. During this lecture he asserted that our marriage wouldn't work if I didn't trust him. He justified the garbage by assuring me that his parents were paying him back for his meals out – I doubt he ever asked them.

We purchased a calorie counting book at Barnes and Noble so that I was able to log my food and calories throughout the day. I was allotted 1,500 calories per day so that I was in a constant calorie deficit. Soon, he had me handing in my log in the evening so he could help keep me on track. I began working out more rigorously and the weight came off.

When I was not within my 'ideal weight range', Ian let me know it. The punishments didn't start quite yet, but the precursors were there. The derogatory comments during sex increased, he began to pressure me for sexual acts that I was not comfortable with, and he started only having sex with me from behind because he was 'disgusted' by my body. When he got off, he would hand me a towel to clean up and then leave to go play video games.

It wasn't all bad, however. Every now and then, he would apologize for one or two transgressions.

"Baby, I love you so much, you are what saved my life and you are the love of my life. I'm so sorry I am short with you sometimes; I really am sorry."

Between his apologies and our church speaking about Christian marriages, I assumed that we were just a normal couple dealing with normal stuff. These times I would renew my resolve to be a better wife.

One of the career paths that Ian chose was massage therapy which was great for me because I got free massages. At first, they were Swedish massages, relaxing and disarming. He would practice new techniques on me as he progressed with his education. Once he learned trigger point therapy, he ran with it. I winced with each trigger point that he dug his knuckles in to.

"Just breathe, it will take the pain away. This is necessary though."

He left bruises all over me in the name of health. He began to cover my back in creams that were meant to relax your muscles, but they had the opposite effect. I am very sensitive if not allergic to these creams. He would complete his trigger point therapy and then watch as I suffered.

When he graduated, he began working at a large bougie gym in our town. He started out as a towel boy and then moved up to massage therapist. Both of us benefited from free memberships. My routine was the same every day –

treadmill, elliptical, stair stepper, floor workout, and stretching. By this time, we had decided that when I was between 193lbs and 197lbs I still had 'excess weight' on my body. We agreed that my new range would be 185lbs to 189lbs.

We both decided to get heart rate monitors so that we could be aware of the calories that we burned in a day. The one that I got had a small sensor on an elastic band which sat just below my bra line. The watch that came with it reflected the calories that I had burned in a day. Soon, Ian became suspicious of my workouts. He was convinced that I was slacking and lying about the number of calories I was burning. He began to wear the watch that corresponded to my sensor so he could see that I was burning *at least* 800 calories per day.

Despite my caloric intake dropping to 1,200 calories per day and actively burning at least 800 calories per day, I struggled to lose the 'podge' that was on my lower stomach. Ian talked to a personal trainer about me and asked her how I could get rid of it. She told him it was normal. He accused me of manipulating her to say that. I had never met her before.

Every now and then I would find the energy to speak with him about his control. These conversations would turn into the dreaded lectures assuring me that he just wanted to live long and healthy lives together because he couldn't live without me.

"Don't you think my doctor would tell me if I was overweight? I really don't think I am."

He replied with the same answer every time, "Doctors can't tell you the truth because they can get sued for malpractice, so they can't tell you that you are overweight even though you are."

He set up a time for me to see one of the male personal trainers. The trainer told me that he was aware of our goal for my lower stomach and then reluctantly set me up for a workout routine that would reduce, if not eliminate, the dreaded 'podge'.

ANNIKA ROSE

Isolated

Age 22-25

Ian stopped taking me around our friends because I embarrassed him with my 'humor' and 'stupidity'. Also, apparently his friends were embarrassed *for* him because I was the ugliest spouse in the group. When I didn't come around anymore, he told them that I was sick/working/tired/etc.

I was fully isolated. I was convinced that my family was toxic, that my friends were fake, and that it was all because I was a flawed human being. The only people I had access to were Ian, my boss, his parents, and very rarely, our friends.

Three years into our marriage, I was promoted to manage one of our newer salons. I was working very hard for a promotion and spent most of my time at work. When I wasn't at work, I was working out, and I had gotten down to around 175lbs. The new rule was that I had to stay between 175lbs and 179lbs. I was exhausted all the time and my clothes were falling off. That wasn't too much of a problem though because his mom kept buying me new wardrobes.

Ian came home one day in a particularly down mood. After a little prying, he divulged that he got fired from the gym because they were too slow to have 5 massage therapists. (I would later find out that he was fired for sexual harassment of a client).

We couldn't afford memberships anymore, so I started working out at our apartment's workout room and in our living room. Ian decided he wanted to be a paralegal, so he started at the community college to finish his associates degree before continuing to his four-year degree.

I lived to please him and avoided upsetting him. When my weight was not adequate, punishments became a part of our life. They ranged from the cold shoulder, to threatening divorce, to sex withheld or conversely, rape. I wore only a thong to sleep in so he could assess my body as I walked around the king-sized bed to lay down. He was monitoring the skin between my hip bones, if it protruded past my hipbones, I was punished.

I was unable to lose any more weight once I hit 170lbs and 14% body fat. At that time, we began talking about getting my hip bones shaved down. I was empty, a shell of who I once was.

I tried to like our sex. The church believed that once married, your body belongs to your spouse, but I was dying of safe touch deprivation. When he was in the mood, he threw me on the bed and angrily fucked me until he got off on my tears.

Outside of the bedroom, life trudged on. I felt like I was walking through knee deep mud in a fog covered swamp. Everything was slow, my heart pounded out of my chest when I worked out, and I suffered from extreme muscle cramping. When I sat on the toilette, my pelvic bones balanced on the seat causing bruises to the thin layer of skin that covered them. It was worth it though because I was 'healthy'.

He was accepted to the 4-year college in 2008. He began to make new friends and spend a lot of time at school. The law classes he was taking taught him more manipulation tactics. One of the requirements of his schooling was that he volunteered a certain amount of time per semester. He chose to be a legal advocate for a domestic violence shelter, 'helping' women navigate the legal system. His volunteering blocked me from seeking help if I ever would have realized how abusive he was.

I filled over 5 journals front to back by then and kept them in my bedside table. Ian felt that I was withholding things from him when I wrote in my journals and that equated to 'putting a bullet in our marriage'. I tried to explain that I needed somewhere to fully express my emotions but he pressed on by calling me a liar and asserting that I might as well be cheating on him.

One day I couldn't hold back my frustration,

"You wouldn't like what is in there, it's all just stupid feelings from when I'm on my period. They don't mean anything."

He pushed further and I lost it. I pulled the drawer out of the nightstand and dumped all my journals on the floor,

"FINE! Read them! Go for it, but it's not my fault if what you read makes you mad!!"

I'm not sure if he ever read them but I know I stopped writing them. He had stolen the last piece of privacy and fully destroyed my dignity as an independent woman.

One night I had a random dream that a fellow salon manager came to me and said,

"I'm not going back to jail."

I was confused but brushed it off when I woke up. Later that day I got a call from my Franchisee.

"Are you sitting down?"

My heart sunk "Is it Damon?"

She paused, "How did you know?"

I insisted, "What happened to him?"

She told me that he had gotten into a fight with his ex-girlfriend, and she stabbed him in the chest, and he passed away. I collapsed on the floor; through sobs I told her,

"I had a dream last night where he said he wasn't going back to jail."

We were both in shock about his death.

I went home and told Ian about what had happened. I struggled for a few days with my grief, naturally, but I was shocked when Ian accused me of cheating with Damon. He thought I had to have been sleeping with Damon in order to be devastated and grieving his death. Up until this point, I had not realized the depth of Ian's jealousy.

At this point, I'd lost everything. He controlled my money, body, voice, behavior, social connections, coping mechanisms, driving (had a tracker on my car), home environment, work connections, and my mind.

People ask me why I didn't leave. I didn't leave because I believed that God meant for marriage to last a lifetime. I had made a commitment and I intended to keep that promise – for better or worse – and this was the worse. I did, however, pray that God would kill me in my sleep every night.

There was an aspect of myself that I had always noticed but never entertained because it was deemed 'satanic' by the church. I had premonitions. I've had them since I was little, but never talked about it. At the beginning of

2009 I had a chronic nagging thought that I was going to have a medical crisis that would change every part of my life. I finally told my mom about it just to see if I could finally get it out of my head. It remained a nagging feeling.

I went into 'beast mode' at work, cutting hair all the time, managing everything in my life, working well over 60 hours per week while only getting paid for 40 hours - if that. Ian was at college full time, so it was chaotic.

I was not conscious of the fact that I was being abused. I was brainwashed to think that all our rules and consequences were my choosing and consequences of my actions. I was convinced that if I worked harder and got thinner that he would be more kind. It never occurred to me that he wasn't upholding his responsibilities as a Christian husband.

That Escalated Quickly

Age 25

In summer of 2009 we went to his cousin's wedding. I was at my lowest weight, 175 pounds, and was excited to dress up and let my hair down a little. I wanted so desperately for Ian to be proud to have me on his arm.

In the hotel bathroom I was getting ready for the day and Ian told me how beautiful I was, my heart swelled with relief. He started to kiss me lovingly, and gently laid me on the bed. What I didn't realize was that my head was just barely separated from the headboard. His kind demeanor faded, and his eyes went black. The top of my head was smashed into the headboard over and over again. I tried to move down, but he wouldn't let me. He said it was hot. I started to tear up, but he went until he got off, hopped up and said we had to go. I shook it off, put my shoes on, and met up with his family for pictures.

Throughout the evening, he barely paid attention to me. I sat with his cousins on the outskirts of the dance floor as he twirled around with everyone but me. The bruise that was under my curly hair started to throb and I wished I was in the room sleeping. I attempted to talk about it later in the evening, but he wasn't having it. We both went to bed silently ignoring each other.

Back at home I was helping to open a new salon with our franchisee which took a lot of work outside of normal business hours. I was chosen to be the manager of the new salon so the pressure was on. I had worked 14 days in a row and finally had a day off, so I put my swimsuit on and went out to the lawn to lay in the sun before Ian and I went out to dinner. As I laid in the warmth of the summer sun, my head began to spin and confusion set in. I went inside to drink some water, assuming I was dehydrated. When the fog didn't pass, we decided to head to dinner early so that I could get some food in me and hopefully relieve the vertigo.

We arrived at the restaurant, parked the car, and both got out. The restaurant was to the left of us and a strip mall was to the right. I intended to go left to the restaurant, but my body took me toward the strip mall.

Ian got irritated and laid into me about needing to stay hydrated and I relented because I was too dizzy to fight back.

Even though I drank copious amounts of water and exceeded my 500-calorie allotment at dinner, I still felt horrible for the rest of the evening. I went to bed early hoping that sleep would be the answer.

My alarm came sooner than I expected. I wiped the sleep from my eyes as I tip toed to the bathroom, gingerly closing the door behind me in an effort to leave Ian sleeping. He wouldn't wake up until around 8:00am so this was a rare time that I was able to have my guard down.

I took a look in the mirror, critiquing the body I was trained to hate, then sat down on the toilet. I took a deep breath and let my lower stomach muscles relax, noticing my 'podge' was no longer a 'podge'. The skin over my lower stomach protruded about an inch past my hip bones, solely because I have human organs stored in there. I noticed the sharp pressure of the seat digging into my pelvic and hip bones, but I was too tired to care.

BANG!

Suddenly the door swung opened and Ian stormed in, infuriated. He looked at me and started yelling,

"YOU LIED TO ME!!"

My adrenaline spiked and I sat in frozen confusion. My body turned to ice as I watched the blood rush from his chest, up his neck, and into his face. The only thing I could utter was,

"What are you talking about?"

Then I realized that when he came in, I had my lower stomach relaxed.

"Get on the scale. NOW."

I was not going to do that, not so much because I was being stubborn, but because I couldn't move. When I refused to get onto the scale, he stormed out of the room and began to pace the hallway and living room. My confusion quickly gave way to a rage I'd never felt before.

Totally nude, I followed him to the living room. We faced off from opposite sides of the room, both flooded with adrenaline.

He started in, "You are lucky that I am with you! You are an embarrassment, a failure! Even my parents hate that I am with you."

I tried to respond, "That's not…"

He cut me off. "I've lowered the bar so low that I might as well not even have standards anymore, and you aren't even hitting *that* bar."

Ice filled my veins and a fire ignited in my brain, "NO! It's MY turn to talk, you've been talking for SEVEN years. Now it's MY turn."

Who is this woman? Certainly not me?

I continued, "LOOK AT ME!!! I am 6 feet tall, a size 8, 34C boobs, long blonde hair, and I can't think of 1 man who wouldn't be PROUD to be with me! I don't have a weight problem; YOU HAVE A PROBLEM WITH MY WEIGHT!!!"

We both stood there in silence, stunned.

Before he could retort, I turned on my heels, walked back to the bathroom and continued getting ready for work. The adrenaline drained through my feet into the ground leaving me fuzzy and numb. I got dressed, grabbed my purse, walked right past him, and left for work.

I arrived at the salon, unlocked the door, and turned the lights on. This space was bigger than the salon I previously managed. As I walked the length of the room, there were stations on my left and on my right, and at the far end was my office to the left, and the breakroom to the right.

I went to the breakroom, put my 2 hardboiled eggs and half cup of egg salad in the mini fridge, and settled in my office for a minute. I checked the schedule, got the money out of the safe, and dropped my purse off under my desk before opening the register.

I was setting up my shears and clippers, making sure I had enough sanitizer and clipper spray when I noticed the line of people outside the door. It was 7:50am, ten minutes before opening.

We opened the doors at eight. I got people checked in to the computer and then welcomed a lovely older man into my chair. He had a style that I could cut in my sleep so I kind of fell into autopilot, thinking over the fight, word by word.

I came back into the conversation when the doorbell rang. I turned my attention back to my client who continued on,

"…yeah, so she won't be there, but we will still have a good time."

I realized I didn't know what he was talking about. Oops. I tried to catch up, begging my brain to recall anything he had said.

"Mhmm", "Oh yeah?" I was failing, and he knew it.

I went to change my clipper blade and my hand felt like clay, not quite numb, but also not connected to me. *Geez, I must be more tired than I thought!* I continued to fade his hair, the methodical buzzing noise comforting, it felt like home. A couple of minutes later my ears started ringing so loud that the busy salon became muffled, and a fog progressively clouded my brain.

Jesus Christ, keep it together… just until the end of this cut… for the love of God.

Just as I finished his final touches my vision blurred, and the world started spinning under my feet. I turned and grabbed one of my staff to collect payment and I started toward the back of the salon. I wandered around the 8' by 12' break room knowing that I wanted something, but not sure what it was, or where it was at.

Maybe it's a low blood sugar? I went to the fridge to grab my egg salad. I turned around and noticed I had grabbed my hard-boiled eggs instead. *Okay, change of plans, no biggie, I just needed some paper towels… wait… where were they again?* I asked a stylist where they were and she pointed them out – they were right where they had always been, hanging from the shelf directly in front of me. She cocked her head, her confusion turned to concern and she had me sit down. She asked me to explain how I felt.

"Um… ummm……. I um, I can't… I don't know."

There is a long history of strokes and heart attacks in my family, so I wanted to call my dad to ask him if my symptoms were more than dehydration. The stylist helped me to my office, and I called him. After sharing the symptoms with him, he confirmed my fear.

"Honey, it sounds like you are having a stroke. You need to get to the nearest hospital immediately."

An Overwhelmed System

Age 25

I grabbed my purse and keys and started slowly walking up to the front of the salon. I was off balance, but I figured that I was just going to be sitting while driving, and I needed to get to the hospital.

With slow speech I called over my shoulder, "Ok girls, I'll be back once I get checked out, I'm sure it's nothing. Thank you so much for covering."

They were not having it. Two of them came and sat me down in a chair.

"There is no way you are driving yourself to the hospital. Can you call your husband?"

I was terrified to call Ian, I knew he blamed me for feeling sick the night before and then the blow up this morning, this wasn't going to go well. I realized there was no other choice, so I called him.

"Hey, I'm not doing so well."

"Shocker. What's wrong this time?" his sarcasm was not lost on me.

"Ian, can you come get me? I think I am having a stroke and I need to go to the hospital…"

"We discussed this last night. You are just dehydrated. Between the gas for me to get there and the hospital bill, you are shooting us in the foot financially."

"I don't know what to tell you, my staff won't let me drive."

He showed up to the salon 45 minutes later. I was sitting in my office with my head down on my desk when Sarah came back and told me that he was outside honking the horn. Sarah and Brittany helped me walk to the truck and get in the passenger side.

The silence was deafening as we rode to the urgent care. By the time we got there, I was having a hard time walking as my left side began to shut down.

The doctor took one look and said he couldn't do much, and it may be serious, so he told us to go to the hospital.

Ian warmed up a bit as he realized that it probably was not dehydration. He saw an opportunity to be the martyr, the doting husband, the puppeteer. We walked from the truck into the emergency department. I clung to the rail on the wall, my left side markedly weaker than my right, slowly following behind him.

"Don't be dramatic" he whispered.

Tears began to roll down my cheeks, I was confused, and my body was failing me.

The triage nurse began her battery of diagnostic questions. She suspected a stroke but was unable to get me the meds that would stop it because the window of time had passed – the symptoms started the night before when I got out of the car to go into the restaurant.

The ER that we were at was in a rough area of the city so my case fell behind gun-shot victims and ambulance bay cases. Meanwhile, I sat in the waiting room, slowly decompensating while he began to call our family, letting them know that something was *really* wrong, and they should come to the hospital.

During the next 8 hours I had an MRI, a CT scan, X-rays, and a lumbar puncture. The scans came back free of any brain anomalies or vascular issues, but the spinal tap wouldn't come back for over 12 hours. By this time Jennifer and Ian's parents had arrived at the hospital and were trying to keep my spirits up, but it was difficult as my speech slowed and my reaction time lengthened. Late in the night, they admitted me from the ER to the stroke unit. Though I had not had a stroke, they didn't have anywhere else that was appropriate.

Ian slept in the bed next to me each night and our moms spent all of visitor's hours either next to my bed or dealing with insurance and setting up my leave of absence from work. For 4 days, I was doing occupational therapy and speech therapy because we didn't know if the functional deficits were going to persist.

Each day the symptoms got worse. By day 3 I was speaking at about a quarter of my normal speed and my coordination was almost gone. I was also unable to get my legs to work, so I could not walk on my own. I was eating warm cereal and meal replacements because my reaction time had slowed to the degree that I couldn't react if I was choking on food. Ian continued to keep a tally on how many calories I was consuming because I wasn't exercising at all during my time in the hospital.

On the fourth day, during a rare moment of being alone in my room, a neurologist came in to talk to me. After explaining that they couldn't quite figure out what was going on, he ended the conversation with what he thought was a joke.

"Well, I guess we are going to have to put you in a nursing home, but you will be the youngest one there! Ha-ha!"

I was pissed, *T.h.i.s i.s. b.u.l.l.s.h.i.t.*

I decided I was done with this; I did not have time for this, and I was going to will my body to work. As I tried to get out of the bed, I was lucky that Ian walked in to catch me before I fell on my face. After that comment, my mother-in-law decided that was enough, so she made a call to someone she knew at the Mayo Clinic and we got in the car to go get a second opinion.

I slept during the three-hour drive and was woken up when we arrived in the emergency department bay. They got me in quickly and reviewed all the studies that the other hospital had done. I went through interview after interview until a short inquisitive man came in and sat on a chair in front of me.

He looked at me with a sympathetic, almost patronizing, demeanor.

"Are you saaaad?"

I got angry, "N.o., I.m. P.i.s.s.e.d."

He continued to ask about my home environment and work. Ian admitted that he had been pretty hard on me and feigned regret. He shared just enough to validate our family's suspicion that he was controlling me, but not enough to be the truth. I shared how much I worked and told them my diet and work out habits.

To my surprise, my biological mom popped her head into the room and came to give me kisses and snuggles. She had flown all the way from California to Minneapolis, and then took a cab the three hours to the Mayo Clinic. I was so overwhelmed that my speech slowed again, and I struggled to express that

I was so happy she was there. Her smell was such a comfort, and I knew Ian couldn't hurt me while she was there. I drifted off to sleep once she sat down at my bedside.

I was not privy to the drama that ensued outside of my room. I later found out that Ian had convinced everyone that she was dangerous and that my slowed speech meant that I didn't want her there. I woke up and asked for her and they said she was gone. I panicked inside but couldn't express it to them. She apparently put up a fight and security got involved. The next thing I knew, she was banned from the hospital and was on her way back to California.

After about 12 hours, we finally got a diagnosis: Conversion Disorder. They said that because I had so many stressors at home and at work, my brain couldn't handle the load anymore and put the stress onto my body. They said once the stress was relieved, I would regain my bodily function.

They were looking for a unit that had an open bed and offered me the option of the psych ward, or the psych medical floor which would be more nurturing to my situation. With the input of Ian and our families, we decided on the psych medical floor. They rolled my bed down hallway after hallway, each one narrower and dimmer. We finally turned the corner and from my gurney I could see to my left, security guards, and to my right what I could best describe as holding rooms. They were 5'x10' psych rooms with plate glass over everything, the only thing that can be grabbed onto is a red panic button. As we approached my holding room, my chest felt like it had caught fire, and then I felt like a semi-truck had driven from my groin to my neck. I was still moving very slow and was speaking even slower, so it was very difficult to explain how I was feeling

I managed to say, "I. t.h.i.n.k. I.m. h.a.v.i.n.g. a.n. a.l.l.e.r.g.i.c. r.e.a.c.t.i.o.n."

I needed help. The nurse ignored me, I could see the pained look on Jennifer's face as she helplessly walked next to me. They turned me into the room feet first, mom and Ian followed, and then they shut the door. I was in a full panic attack. I wanted to quit.

"T.A.K.E. M.E. H.O.M.E. I.M. D.O.N.E.!"

No one would listen. Mom kept rubbing my hair, trying to comfort me, and Ian didn't know what to do so he spaced out on the other side of the tiny room. My bones were digging into the hard board under the 1.5 inches of foam on my gurney. Mom tried to advocate for an anti-anxiety med, but they didn't respond. Finally, by about 3:00am, they opened the door, and rolled me down to the psych floor where I was kept in a room with a camera that watched me sleep, alone, with the lights on. I was terrified.

Through fits and starts, I slept. At about 6:00am, I woke up and had to pee. I called the nurse,

"U.m. I. N.e.e.d. t.o. u.s.e t.h.e b.a.t.h.r.o.o.m."

"Well get up and pee then…"

I told her I couldn't walk on my own, and then we both realized I was on the wrong floor. I was supposed to be on the Medical Psych floor, not the Psych floor. She came and helped me, I ate some oatmeal, and then the doctor wrote orders to move my room to the other floor.

Once moved, a whole team of doctors came into my room and asked me questions for what seemed like forever. When they left, I had to go to a DBT (dialectical behavior therapy) class which I basically slept through, then lunch which I didn't eat because I didn't know what the calories were.

Jennifer and Ian came to visit during the visiting hours. They told me that my leave had been approved. I was so relieved to have a break from the rat race I had been sucked in to, so much so, that my speech began to speed up. Ian cried and apologized for putting so much pressure on me, disarming both my mom and I, the relief made my leg function increase. The doctors had asked me what makes me happy, and I told them that I loved animals. Ian then promised to get me a kitty.

At this point, I had started to come back to normal – with some deficits – but enough for the doctors to feel my symptoms could be managed at home. My discharge instructions included seeing a therapist multiple times per week close to home, not driving, and not working for the foreseeable future, as well as getting an animal and doing things that make me happy.

The aftermath of the conversion was hard for everyone to deal with. I was reduced to tears at the slightest thing and was exhausted 24/7. Every time I was too stressed, the conversion symptoms would reoccur.

ANNIKA ROSE

Realizations and Consequences

Age 25

When I was released from the hospital, I started to see the follow up therapist. Twenty minutes in to our first session, she referred me back to the eating disorder program I had been in when I was younger. She said it was to go to a 'stress management' class where they already had records on me. This was brilliant. She realized that I was dangerously entrenched in my eating disorder and that my husband was a driving factor in it.

We made an appointment for an initial assessment for a week later. The appointment included an EKG, labs, and more talking. I thought it was a bit excessive for a stress management class, but that was the new policy at the facility. After the tests came back, she said that I was malnourished and had all the symptoms of advanced anorexia. Ian was in the room, and I could see in his eyes that he strongly disagreed.

I froze. His stance had always been that doctors will never tell you that you are fat even though you are because of malpractice suits. I was in disbelief.

"You've got to be joking."

Her face was serious and persuasive, "Your heart is severely fatigued, your liver enzymes are off, and your kidneys are shutting down. Did you pack a bag?"

Why would I pack a bag for an intake for a stress management class?

"I would like to admit you to the third floor."

I had no idea what that meant.

"It's the inpatient section of the facility, just until we can get your heart a little stronger and get your labs better."

I looked to Ian; his eyes had turned black. This was not lost on her. She asked him to leave the room to finish the conversation. Once alone, I told her that I was willing if I wasn't the biggest one on the unit. She assured me that I wasn't, so I agreed.

When the doctor left to get the paperwork ready, Ian lectured me, "Remember, these people get paid to make you fat. Go through the motions, but do not let them make you gain weight – remember our promise to eat less and work out…"

I felt like a tennis ball, going back and forth between a doctor I had never met and the man that would be keeping me accountable for a promise I made years ago that was clearly killing me.

I was admitted later that day to the spacious unit. Ian's mother helped me set up my side of the room with my own blanket, photos, and my comfy clothing. Once everyone left, it was silent in my room. So much had flipped upside down in the last 12 hours and I was spaced out.

I had to adjust to the supervised bathroom use, nurses checking my vitals three times per day, seeing a doctor before sunrise, and being on activity restrictions. The hardest part was the 3 meals and 3 snacks per day. We were called to the dining room which was a moderately sized room with two large glass topped tables. Our meals were brought up from the kitchen and we were expected to eat everything that was given to us. I could hear Ian in the back of my mind. This was not good.

I was discharged after nine days on the unit; my vitals were stabilizing, and I was compliant with all of the requests made of me. I was transitioned into partial inpatient treatment which was on the second floor. I was at the facility 12 hours per day, 6 days per week. By the end of the summer, I had gained around 11 pounds and Ian was furious.

I had been working with my eating disorder therapist for over a month. I started to accept that my 'eating healthy and working out' lifestyle had turned into anorexia and that Ian was enforcing it. I was also surprised to find out that Ian may actually be abusive. My therapist taught me about the cycle of abuse. I could see Ian and I going around and around: build up, explosion, apologies, honeymoon, build up, explosion, apologies, honeymoon.

About a week before Labor Day, I sat Ian down and told him that we needed to talk.

I looked him straight in the face, "The relationship we have is abusive, Ian. I don't see how we can fix this. I ask you for what I need, you apologize and tell me you will change, and then you do the same thing again."

I was tired of his parents covering for him and exhausted with consistently being in trouble with him.

Flatly I continued, "I don't see how our marriage can work anymore."

He went to his knees, "No, no, no, baby, I can't live without you, I know I've been a terrible husband, but I promise I will be better. I'm so sorry!"

Tears streamed down his face as he made the plea of a lifetime. I was exhausted with all of it and my brain slowed with the stress. I shared how we fit into the domestic violence cycle. He sat quietly, listening intently, apparently taking it all in. After he listened to me for an hour or so, his parents came home and we had the talk with them about the thoughts I was having. I was on the fence.

Is he really going to change? If he is, I need to keep my commitment, it wouldn't be fair not to.

The next day, his parents sat us down and proposed an idea that we thought might just work.

"We want to send you on a second honeymoon to Duluth, MN for Labor Day weekend. We want you to be able to reconnect and strengthen your foundation again."

I reluctantly agreed. I was still in treatment 5 days per week for 8 hours per day, so I processed the last 24 hours with my groups and individual therapist. There was a small voice in the back of my head saying that this is very bad, he could kill me and make it look like an accident.

Before I left, I made emergency plans with a friend's parents in case he decided to hurt me in some way. I didn't end up needing the back up because he was charming. He reassured me about my weight, gave me grace regarding workouts and was accommodating in everything. I was starting to think that things were getting better.

ANNIKA ROSE

New York, New York

Age 26

Two weeks after our second honeymoon, I got clearance from my treatment team to take an 8-day trip to New York City with Jennifer. My treatment team and I planned everything from possible triggers all the way down to the times that I was going to eat. The one thing that I was not prepared for was Ian's reaction to not being invited.

In the days leading up to the trip, Ian went on a marathon of monologues basically stating how my family is toxic and that his parents would never just take one of us on a trip. He tried to pit me against my family again, but I wasn't having it. His parents went so far as to join in on the campaign to either keep me home or have Ian join. They did not count on the fact that my mom was just as stubborn as they were, and that I was finally finding my voice.

Our time in NYC was amazing. We saw *Chicago* on Broadway, ate the BEST cheesecake of my life at Roxy's in Time Square, and I experienced the most positive male attention that I had ever in my life. I was floored, I had told Ian that any man would be happy to be with me, but I had no idea that I was really perceived as beautiful, sexy even. I was still underweight, but I was making progress. I ate somewhat normally while on this trip – I enjoyed pancakes again for the first time in *years* and the only guilt that I felt was that Ian was at home pouting.

ANNIKA ROSE

Same Old, Same Old

Age 26

The abuse cycle raged on when I got home. The full cycle would span about a month each time, but it was the same merry-go-round. I finally saw it for what it was immediately after I got home, but I wasn't able to stop it.

Ian was bright eyed and excited when I arrived at the house. "Honey I am so glad you are home. I missed you so much, tell me all about your trip."

"It was great, we had an amazing time, but I missed you. We should go some day!"

A few days later, he became cold and distant, silently judging everything that I put into my mouth. "What are you eating, are you sure you aren't going over your tallies?"

I was gaining strength as I continued treatment and increased my ability to push back. "I'm doing exactly as my dietician and doctor are telling me. They aren't lying to me; they are helping me get healthy."

Again, Ian was silent for days. In a subconscious effort to ease the tension, I began to restrict calories here and there.

I appealed to him, "What's wrong? Did I do something? I'm sorry if I did."

He didn't respond until midnight when I had already taken my night medication and was falling asleep. He was on the opposite side of the king-sized bed.

"I can't believe you've done this to me. You trapped me. You were attractive when we got married, and now I couldn't lower the bar more. I didn't sign up for this. I understand for better or worse, sickness and health and all of that, but I made that contract under false pretenses. I can either stay with you and be miserable, or be single and be miserable, I don't know which one would be worse.

I was worn down, feeling dejected and ashamed, "I am so sorry, I know that I'm supposed to be a respectful wife, and that God calls me to be your helper, and I know I'm not helping you right now. What I really want for us, is to have a supportive relationship. I want you to love me for who I am, not what I look like. I miss you; I miss our touch; I miss the love you used to show me."

Ian, increasingly irritated, "You aren't the victim here, don't try to make me feel bad for having standards and expecting that my wife stays consistent. Excuse me for wanting to be attracted to my wife. If you think it would be different with any other man, you are wrong. Only in romcoms do people fall in love without the prerequisite of attraction. I've done everything you need. You don't think that it has been hard on me AND my parents having you like this? You are joking yourself if you do. You are ungrateful for what my family has done for you."

I just wanted to sleep, but tears streamed down my face, "I am so sorry, I didn't realize I was hurting you too."

By this point I was broken down and right where he wanted me. I hated that this was happening and I was convinced it was my fault because I was broken and worthless.

Once Ian realized that I was resigned, he softened and pulled me in to him, "I know baby, we just need to try harder to adhere to the rules that we made so that our marriage can work. I want you to be healthy so we can grow old together."

Just wanting to go to sleep, I conceded. "I promise babe, I'll work harder."

By December, we had gone around this cycle at least three times, all with the same message, all with the same false hope at the end.

At Christmas, Ian wouldn't even look at me, let alone touch me. I would try to cuddle up to him, but he would grunt and turn his back to me. I finally asked what was wrong and he said that I was so disgusting that he couldn't look at me. *Here we go again.*

"Ian, you expect perfection, and I just can't maintain that."

He rolled his eyes as I continued, "Maybe you should look at your standards and determine if they are realistic or not."

I knew what his answer to that was, but it was devastating each time.

"I might as well not have any standards; the bar can't get any lower than it already is. You wonder why we don't have sex anymore? I can't do it unless my eyes are closed and I'm fantasizing about another woman."

I had gained about 30 pounds since the beginning of treatment and was still quite thin. I decided to speak to his mom about the problem, hoping that she would empathize and speak to him since my words clearly weren't working. Her response shocked me,

"Well, are you even happy with your body since you gained weight? He might be justified."

During the conversation, Ian came up the stairs and sat down with us. He told his mom that he couldn't 'get it up'. She suggested he see his primary care physician and he looked at her blankly,

"No, I don't struggle with my erections, I just can't get turned on looking at her."

His mom didn't know what to say, "Well, this will pass, all marriages go through hard times."

ANNIKA ROSE

2 Steps Forward, 1 Back

Age 26

I began severely restricting again, eating about 30% of the meal plan that was prescribed to me. My behavior, and Ian's response to my body persuaded my providers to admit me again to inpatient treatment. They needed to get me away from him so I could do what I needed to get better. Unfortunately, my uncle passed away a few days before my admission and I had to miss his funeral – this disorder and Ian were taking everything from me.

Ian only came to the unit a couple of times during this stay. He was sweet again and one afternoon, just wanted to take a nap with me. Since we were married, he was allowed to be in my room with the door closed. We began to fall asleep, and he started to kiss my neck.

"No Ian, not here."

I was on a movement restriction, meaning that I could only walk in the hallways, but could not do anything strenuous. I could either sit, lay down, or walk to the dining room.

"Honey, we haven't had sex in forever and I really just want to connect with you."

He pressed on. I went numb and escaped into the void. It took about 5 minutes for him to get off and wipe himself off with my tee-shirt. I was beet red, partially because I was malnourished and partially because I had just had sex and had to hide it from the nursing staff.

At the end of January, they transferred me across the hall to the residential treatment wing, where the medically stable people go that are still struggling with behaviors. I was learning how to live without an eating disorder, and I needed to focus. There was a major shift in Ian's attitude. He completely checked out. I did everything that I could in the couple of times that he visited me to make him happy, but he just pushed me away.

Knocked Off Center

Age 26

On the morning of February 13th, shortly after our 7:00am breakfast, I was knitting and talking to other patients in the day room when my therapist came to get me. We didn't have an appointment, so I was confused… there must be something wrong. She took me into one of the group rooms.

"Hailey, your insurance has decided that they cannot pay for your residential treatment anymore, and they are only paying until 8:00 tomorrow morning."

I went numb, *how am I supposed to do this at home?? I am not ready!*

I just looked at her. She knew my fears, and she knew that my health was severely jeopardized at home.

"I think it would be helpful if you went home with Ian for an 8-hour pass so that you are able to discuss arrangements and how you plan to move forward with your recovery as an outpatient."

"Okay, but I need to call the insurance company first."

I got the community phone and called. I feel very bad for the woman on the other end of the phone. She told me there is nothing they can do and I hung up the phone with a flaming,

"IT'S ON YOU IF I DIE FROM THIS DISEASE."

I dreaded the next call – to Ian.

"Honey, so, here's the deal…"

I explained everything and he said he wasn't ready for me to come home, that he was still working on himself.

"Where do you think I should go? I have nowhere else."

"Maybe we should talk to your mom…"

Was I being kicked out of my home?

He came to pick me up around 9:30am. I would have lunch and afternoon snack with him, and he would bring me back before dinner. It was supposed to be a valentine's date, but Ian cancelled the movie, and we got ice cream instead, which he criticized.

We went home mid-afternoon to start packing what I would need at my mom's house. I didn't know how long I would be there, so I packed two weeks' worth of clothes and toiletries. I stood at the bed, looking over my suitcase, bawling.

Ian responded to my show of emotion coolly, "This is for the best baby, you know this. We are both unhealthy and we need to get better to be a better couple."

I understood where he was coming from.

Before we brought my things upstairs, he kissed me passionately, then bent me over the bed and railed me. One last time for good measure, I suppose.

I arrived back to the facility exhausted. I didn't talk to anyone, I walked in a fog from dinner to my room, packed my things and went to sleep, stunned.

I woke up at 6:00am with the nurse at my bedside to collect vitals for the last time in residential, I gathered in the kitchen for breakfast with the other patients for the last time, and I rolled my suitcase down to my therapist's office where Ian was waiting for me.

Our family therapy session started at 8:30am and it did not go anything like I had expected.

Blindsided

Age 26

I met Ian in the waiting room outside of my therapist' office at 8:15am. The air was charged, I knew we needed to talk but the words couldn't find their way out of my mouth. Ian started to mumble, almost to no one,

"Why do I have to talk to your therapist? She's always on your side, this is a waste of time."

The therapist opened the door promptly at 8:30am and motioned for us to come in. I sat on the low seated couch while Ian sat on the throne-like reclining chair across from my therapist.

"How are you guys feeling about Hailey being discharged today? I know it was sudden and not ideal."

She was direct, knowing something was brewing and determined to get to the bottom of it before the 50 minutes expired.

I started, "So we decided that while we both try to get better, it may be helpful for me to go stay with my mom for a bit."

She looked Ian dead in the eyes and challenged him, "Is that right? Whose idea was that?"

She and I both knew that he was my tether to reality, to what dregs of sanity I still had intact and his removal from my life could have dire consequences.

"Well, we talked and I love Hailey to death, but I feel like we are more best friends than soul-mates. I think a separation would be best right now while we figure out where to go next."

Whoa… this is not what we had talked about, at least not what I understood about our conversation. Separation? Best friends? What is happening? I sat in silence while he continued, the sounds in the room becoming muffled and far away.

Forty-five minutes passed as he droned on about how he wants the best for both of us and how my recovery is most important. His circular word salad of a lecture ended with the D word. I came back into myself at the same time that he said "divorce".

"Hailey, what do you think about this?" My therapist looked at me.

"Huh? Um, I can see where he is coming from and if he feels this is best, then I guess it makes sense?"

She nodded, we both had the same realization, he was devastating my life but setting me free at the same time.

After the appointment we drove to his parent's house to get what possessions he deemed were mine. We sat his parents down and told them the news, well Ian told them the news and I sat in disbelief. Tears sprang to his dad's eyes but no words found their way to the surface. I sat, stunned. After a while, his mom stiffened her back,

"Well, I guess that is that." She got up and walked away.

We all got up to say goodbye. Through tears and an extended hug, his dad told me that she was just upset and she didn't mean it. He loved me like his own, and I knew that she did too.

Ian and I went downstairs and I wanted to go through our things to take more with me. He stopped me,

"Honey, we are best friends, you can come over whenever you want and get anything you would like! Today is really hard, do you want to just go rest, and you can come back whenever?"

I agreed.

I don't remember how I got to my mom's house or what happened in the few days that followed. We met that Friday to sign the papers. He directed the conversation and read the stipulations to me as if I was incapable of comprehending legal paperwork. His arrogance knew no bounds. He left me with half of our bank account and anything he decided his parents hadn't paid for.

I was a shell of who I once was. I looked at him, followed the words on the page with my eyes, but nothing was registering. He handed me one of his beloved ink pens and I signed the paper. The next Monday, we met downtown at the courthouse to file the papers officially.

In the end, I retained a television, my clothing, a mirror, my wedding dress, and one night stand. All the crystal from our wedding was gone, all the artwork was his, our bed, all our books, appliances, etc. He took my heart and gave me scraps in return. The bizarre thing was that he seemed fine with it all, there were no tears, no apologies, no deflated mood, nothing. It was as if we had gone on a few dates and then broke up.

Night after night I lay on the floor with my childhood dog sobbing into his fur until I had no breath left. I had never hurt so badly in my life. I came to understand how people die of broken hearts, the physical pain that I felt was indescribable.

ANNIKA ROSE

Major Adjustments

Age 26

Moving home was a culture shock. I found that the childhood home that I grew up in was no longer safe. I quickly came to the realization that Ian had actively destroyed my relationship with my family during our marriage. He had convinced me that my family was toxic and went as far as to have me grieve them as if they had died, while also convincing my family that I was not who they thought they knew. My family thought I was a conceited bitch, but they had no idea the damage that Ian had done.

I was hopeless and lost. I felt untethered to reality. Walking through a haze of uncertainty, I held on to the little hope I had in our friendship. His assurances of communication and contact proved to be a lie. Toward the middle of March, he texted me,

"Stop contacting me, you are being pathetic and I don't need the stress."

I stopped texting and calling and withdrew into my shell.

On the day that our divorce was finalized, Ian posted a few pictures to his social media of himself and a woman at a formal dance. The photos were dated 2/17/2010, three days after he told me we were getting divorced. She was a small mousy woman with long brown hair split down the middle, plain features, and a boyishly slim body. She was clearly younger than me, and I quickly realized it was the Emily that he had spoken about from university.

Under the picture, a caption read, "Look at this hot piece of arm candy, luckiest guy in the world."

The ink was barely dry on our divorce papers. My blood ran cold, my fingers ice cubes as I pulled out my computer. I watched myself open my email and felt my fingers compose the most intense letter I had written to date. Rage flowed down my numbed arms and onto the page, exposing everything that I had just come to terms with. The lying and manipulation, the timing of it all, his perfect façade... I explained how heartbroken I was and that he threw away the best thing he would ever have in this world. I addressed the email to Ian, and then his parents, and mine, then his cousins, and my siblings, basically to everyone I had addresses for. I clicked send.

Sitting in silence I was startled by the guttural scream that escaped my mouth. This sound seemed to be so familiar at this point. My sister came up from her room in the basement and embraced me, her arms the only things holding me together. I had a feeling that he had been cheating but felt guilty for not trusting him. Echoes of his threats flashed through my brain,

"If you don't trust me, how is this marriage supposed to last??"

Flashbacks of the gaslighting and abuse started to come to the surface, but it would take years for me to grasp the depth of the damage that he had done.

Emily had no idea what she had gotten herself into and I didn't care. I didn't know if she knew he was married or not, but at that point, I figured that they deserved each other.

Rebound

Age 26

  The day after finding the photo, my cousin called me and invited me to her friend's birthday party. We would be bar hopping on a party bus. This was a recipe for disaster, and I was there for it.

  The theme was the 80's. I cut the neck out of a sweatshirt so that it would shrug off of my left shoulder, I put my hair in a side ponytail, and then painted my face with bright blue eyeshadow and hot pink lipstick. I was ready to go.

  Once on the bus, we started drinking wine coolers, I was three in when we got to the first bar. (*Bear in mind that I was still underweight and not eating nearly what I should have been for my build.*) Liquor flowed and then came the shots. The amount of male attention was refreshing and confusing at the same time. *Aren't I repulsive? Why are these guys into me??* Three bars and a lot of liquor later, my cousin and I were dropped off at her house. I curled up in her bed and sobbed.

  I woke up the next day to a raging hangover and a text from a guy I had met the night before. I had a hazy memory of what he looked like, then of dancing in his lap, and then of my cousins making sure I didn't go home with him. He was a practice player for our state's NFL team and being next to him made me feel tiny and feminine.

  The rest of the weekend was soaked in wine and vodka. I no longer had Ian to place restrictions on me, and I had no intentions of remembering what had happened with him.

The NFL player and I texted throughout the next week. On Friday, he called me while he was drinking downtown and invited me to meet him. I was hesitant, I wasn't familiar with downtown, nor was I familiar with the party life. After a while, I convinced myself to head down to the bar to meet him. I got there just in time for him to get kicked out for being too intoxicated. Turns out that I was the taxi driver.

He poured himself into the front seat of my corolla and we went to the parking garage that his car was in. He told me he had to get something out of it before we went back to the suburbs where he lived. We drove to the third floor. There were a handful of cars and no people in sight. He pointed out 'his' car. I parked to the left of a cherry red Charger.

I looked out my driver's window and, in my mirrors, to see if anyone was around and when I looked back at him, I noticed that he had pulled his penis out of his pants. He grabbed the back of my head and buried my face in his crotch. I tried to pull away, but he was so strong. The more I pulled the harder grip he had on my hair. I went to another place in my head while he finished in my mouth. When he let go of my hair, I pulled back, opened my door, and threw up on the pavement. By the time I was done, he had passed out in the front seat.

I silently drove to the suburb that he lived in, tears staining my cheeks. I tried to wake him up three to four times for directions, but he was wasted. After driving around for a half hour, I finally got his address out of him. I dropped him off and we didn't speak again.

I went back to treatment the following Monday ashamed and dejected. I told one of the health educators what happened and said I felt like such a slut. Tears welled in her eyes as compassion overtook her.

"Hailey, you know that what he did was assault, right?"

I couldn't accept that. "No, I put myself in that situation. I could have bit down or punched him, I could have done *anything* to prevent it."

"Hailey, rape is NEVER your fault, and you are most certainly not a 'slut'."

Over the next few months, I decided that I was no longer letting Ian ruin my life. I made some integral changes, some glaring mistakes, and began to forge ahead.

Taking My Life Back

Ages 26-28

Two months after the divorce in spring of 2010, Ian graduated with the degree that I supported him in getting. The plan was always for me to start school again once he graduated so I could finish my degree.

After licking my wounds, I decided some things needed to change. I moved from Jennifer's house where I was clearly not welcomed, to my dad's house which was 10 minutes closer to the cities. I decided that if Ian was going to move on, so was I. I applied to university at 26 years old and was accepted. I had 3 years left of my degree due to my abrupt departure from college in 2004, but I was up for the challenge.

Going to school again after I had experienced a marriage, full career, and then divorce, as well as what should have been insurmountable trauma was a shock to my system. Most of the students looked like they were 12 years old and they were into playing frisbie on the quad and binge drinking nightly. I was focused on not failing my classes, staying awake in public areas, and healing.

Every day, I bussed 45 minutes into the campus from my dad's house. I slept on the bus and would *normally* wake up in time to get off the bus at my stop. A couple of times I accidentally slept until the bus's last stop, oops.

My days were spent in class, in my favorite coffee shop, or in this amazing library on campus. I studied constantly, well, when I wasn't falling asleep sitting up.

I was getting plenty of sleep at night but could not keep my brain awake during the day. It didn't matter where I was, in class, on the bus, in line at the coffee shop, etc. I got about a 30 second heads up before my brain just shut down. When I tried to fight it, I would begin to lucid dream and talk in gibberish. I quickly learned that I needed to study where I could take naps head down on the table at least 3 times per day.

At this time, I was not aware that I had dissociative identity disorder, or idiopathic hypersomnolence. I just thought I was dumb and lazy because I couldn't remember anything without falling asleep, taking feverish notes in class, reading every word of the Chapters, and making more notes on that. Even so, there were times in the testing rooms that I would look at the questions and they may as well have been written in Greek − I had no idea what they were asking, let alone what the answer would be.

By pure luck, I was able to pass my classes with B's and C's, which in the moment felt like failure, but looking back, I realize that C's get degrees, and I was doing the best I could with what I was experiencing.

A year into school, my dad's new wife moved in with us from another state where she was selling her house. She and I did not get along, and I began to look for other places to stay where I felt safer.

I began to couch surf, normally with my friends from treatment. These decisions were less than helpful to my recovery, and my impulsive behavior justified their own. Some offered me housing in exchange for rides to the liquor store, while others offered me a room in exchange for nannying services. I also had a few friends who went downtown with me to party, and the worst were the friends who offered me excuses to stay codependent and emmeshed.

It seemed that every time I would get comfortable and was forced to sit with myself, I upended my life. Chaos was my way of coping with the unthinkable, it was my way to protect the denial that was keeping me safe.

Easily swept off my feet, men were able to give me the bare minimum in exchange for the whole of my attention. I was dating at least 3 times per week and was shuffling 3-4 friends with benefits at any given time.

I was in no place to be starting relationships. I hadn't even come to terms with the abuse I had endured in the prior years. I craved the structure that I had in my marriage, even if it was a façade. Ian dictated when I slept, when I ate, what I ate, how much I ate, when I worked, when I worked out, what I said, what I wore, my mannerisms, and my acquaintances. Going from that to pure freedom was a jolt that I was not prepared for.

During my college years, I was in a trauma and survival response loop: eat, drink, sleep, study, date, repeat.

I moved once more while I finished my studies. I met a guy online who was looking for a roommate and was charging far less than I was currently paying for rent. We started talking and he expressed romantic interest in me, however, he was hard core submissive. I am not at all dominant, so we realized it would be a great dynamic, he wasn't dangerous or overbearing, and I was just focused on school.

I moved into his townhome and started to settle in. I was happy with the move, and the rent allowed me a little breathing room. I continued to date, but not as rapidly or recklessly as I had previously.

A year into living with him, he found a significant other with whom he moved in with leaving me to find another roommate. The next roommate was a dog trainer who worked a lot and kept to herself. She was certainly not as outgoing as I am and that caused a bit of friction between us.

I was finally feeling stable financially, relationally, academically, and emotionally... until I took in a roommate who would upend my life, again.

ANNIKA ROSE

Empathy Backfired

Age 28

On a rainy October night in 2012, I was looking at the wanted ads online and noticed a call for help from a woman who was living out of her storage unit after a double stillbirth. My heart broke. I immediately emailed her and set up a time to meet. I didn't know if I could help, but I wanted to support her in some way.

We met the next evening at a coffee shop where she shared her story with me. She was living with her boyfriend who became physically abusive with her while she was pregnant with twins. She ended up having a stillbirth of both babies and afterward, he kicked her out. She was now living out of her storage unit while recovering from his abuse and her physical ordeal.

I hung on every turn that her story took. She went into her family dynamics and her lack of support. My brain began to formulate a plan. The townhome I was living in had a huge dining room that we never used. I had extra-long blackout curtains, and an extra mattress. *Maybe I could create a makeshift room in the townhome so she would have somewhere to stay temporarily?*

I told her that I wanted to help but that I needed to talk to my roommate first. She agreed and emphasized that she can't stay in her storage unit for long because they would kick her out. We wrapped up our conversation and I headed home to have a conversation with my roommate.

I walked in, poured a glass of wine, and sat on the couch. She came into the living room and plopped down on the couch adjacent.

"Hey! How was your coffee meeting?"

"Oh my gosh, I feel so bad for this woman, she was in a domestic violence situation, had stillbirths, and is now living out of her storage unit."

"No way, that's horrible. Doesn't she have any family?"

"No, her mom died 7 years ago, and her dad isn't safe to live with, besides, he lives in another state."

"Oh." She said, realizing what was coming next.

"What do you think about turning the dining room into a third room so she can have a place to stay just for a month while I help her get back on her feet?"

She looked at the ceiling, "Hailey, really?"

"I promise it will only be a month, and I'll have her pay a nominal amount each week and sign a contract."

"I mean, if it's just a month, and it's the holidays, I guess that would be okay, but if anything of mine goes missing, I'm holding you accountable." Her voice was firm.

"Absolutely. I understand where you are coming from and am so grateful you see where I'm coming from too."

I picked up my phone and texted: "Hey Stephanie, I talked to my roommate, and I'm wondering if you want to come stay with us for a month just so you can get back on your feet?"

Within the next three days, I had hung the curtains up to afford her privacy, set up a room for her in the dining room, and wrote up a contract stipulating that she pay $120.00 per week for 4 weeks and that she would be moved out by 1/1/2013.

Stephanie moved in on November 28, 2012 with some clothes and other necessities from her storage unit. I let her set up her vanity on the second sink in my bathroom and tried to help her feel at home. I was trying to ignore the pit in my stomach, but it was overpowering. To quell my fears, I got a copy of her driver's license and her dad's information to add to her contract.

The first night, we sat on my bed, and she showed me a photo of her holding her two stillborn babies in her arms in a hospital bed. I broke down, I couldn't imagine what she had been through. She fed on every tear that I shed seeing it as weakness and stupidity – maybe it was.

After the first week, she had still not paid her weekly rent. She was home all day and didn't seem to be searching for a job at all. The only time that she left was when she had appointments. I didn't press too hard to find out what the appointments were, I just assumed they were medical since her birth was only a month prior.

During the second week I asked her what the appointments were and if she needed help finding a job. She told me that the court needs documents, so she has been running around for those. I pushed past my midwestern passivity,

"What is the court stuff about? Is everything okay?"

A tear came to her eye, "I'll be okay, it's just that I have a restraining order against the baby's dad and it needs to be renewed."

"Oh Stephanie, I'm so sorry. If there's anything I can help with, please let me know."

"Well, there is something. I feel like he may have found me, I keep seeing a car that looks like his driving passed my car in the parking area. Do you think I could use the garage just until I'm out of here? Just so he can't find me?"

"Um, I suppose, are you in any danger?" My anxiety started to mount.

"No, I don't think so. I just need to keep my car off the street and move my storage unit to another location because he has a key to the one I'm in right now."

"Gotcha…"

This was all getting to be a *lot*. It was the holiday season and she had been living with us for two weeks now and there was no rent paid.

The weekend before Christmas, Stephanie told me that she met an amazing man on a dating app a couple weeks ago and had seen him a few times. He agreed to help move her storage units. She asked if I could help too. I reluctantly said yes, even though my back had been bothering me.

Saturday came and I met her new guy, he was a fitness trainer, about my height, and friendly. We knocked out the storage unit in less than an hour and finished the whole project before nightfall.

A few days later, I was sitting at my desk writing when Stephanie walked in and stood in the doorway.

"Hey, can I talk to you about something?"

"Sure, just let me finish this sentence."

She stood there staring at me, "So, you know the guy I'm dating?"

"Yeah…"

"Well, we had sex one time and I'm, well, I'm pregnant."

Stunned, I just looked at her, after an uncomfortable silence I said the only thing I thought was appropriate, "So, are we excited about this? Or…"

I couldn't decide if I should be happy for her or terrified that she is basically homeless with no job and no prospects. She rubbed her belly like she already had a bump.

I felt an uneasiness in my stomach. The timing didn't add up, did it?

"How far along are you?"

They had only been dating for like 3 weeks I thought.

"I don't know how far along; I just know that I took a pregnancy test, and it came back positive. I must still be fertile since I lost the twins only a month ago."

The pragmatic side of me kicked in, "So we need to get you to an OB to start prenatal stuff, right? I don't know how this works."

She smiled, "Yeah, I want to make sure everything is healthy and that everything goes well for this pregnancy."

"Okay, well if there's anything I can do, just let me know."

Christmas came and went and we still had not received any rent. I finally sat her down and had a stern conversation.

"Stephanie, you know that we have a contract for you to stay here, and you have not held up your side of the bargain. I want to help you, but you have to take some personal accountability and handle your obligations. I'm here to help you get on your feet, but you have to actually do the work."

"There's something I need to tell you…" She was nervous. "So, the court stuff… My ex and I *both* have restraining orders against each other, and he's trying to say that I have been texting him and harassing him, so some of the court appointments are for me." A tear leapt from her eye, "I may have texted him a couple of times, but it was just for documents, and now they are trying to serve me for a warrant."

"Oh my God Stephanie! Do you have to go to jail or something?" *What the fuck did I get myself into here??*

"You are *pregnant,* how long are you looking at? How do they handle pregnant women in jail?"

My brain was spinning and I couldn't find my words, my hands were clammy and I felt my heart begin to race.

Calmly she explained, "Well, because it's a misdemeanor, I have to pay a fine before I can go into jail. They need money for room and board before you go."

Okay, that's bullshit… right? People go to jail every day without paying anything…

"It's not a hotel, people go to jail every day without paying anything."

"I don't know, that's just what they told me, and because I don't have a permanent address or a job, I can't pay the fine and they have to wait to put me in jail."

I began to distance myself from her as I realized the shit show that I invited into my life.

January 2013 came and still no payments, no job, and nowhere to live.

I confronted her, "Stephanie, the contract ended on January 1st. You were supposed to be paying each week, which you didn't do, and you were supposed to be moved out by now. My roommate is getting pissed and I don't know what to do."

"Well, you can't kick me out because you have to give 30 days' notice of an eviction."

Oh hell no… "Stephanie," my voice was stern, "I have bent over backward for you. You are not going to pull the eviction shit with me."

Sheepishly, she looked up, "I know, I'm sorry. I'll find somewhere to stay, I promise. Just give me until the 21st."

I took a deep breath, "Fine, but no more than that."

January 21st came, and she hadn't packed anything. "Stephanie, today is it. You can't stay here anymore. My roommate is going to have a fit if you are not gone by the time she gets home from work."

She replied softly, "Ok, I don't know where I'm going to go, but I'll be out. I promise."

As far as I'm concerned, she can go to jail for free housing and food… she just can't stay here.

She did move out that night, and I didn't hear anything from her, or about her, for a few months. I was not sad about that. She took advantage of my kindness and my hospitality. She never paid me anything for rent, and she lied to me about her criminal history.

After Stephanie left the townhome, I focused on the last semester of my bachelor degree journey. My degree was Bachelor of Science in Psychology and

I spent the majority of my time in the research lab working on a pre-existing study with one of my professors.

I finally graduated in May of 2013 with the degree that I had worked so hard to earn. Family came from all over the country to celebrate the accomplishment and I began to plan the next steps.

The next steps were not clear, so I began to nanny for a family near my home and decided to write a book about my experience with anorexia. It was a guide of sorts that would help people who misunderstood eating disorders to understand and be able to support those who were suffering.

All Roads Lead to Dallas

Age 29-30

In March 2014, I was approved for social security disability due to the complex PTSD and conversion disorder. It was such a relief due to the fact that working full time as a caregiver at a group home was too much at that point.

As I was trying to figure out what to do next, I got a random message online from Stephanie's fitness training guy. He explained that she miscarried and took a bunch of money from him, and that he was taking her to court for the loss. Somehow, I was not surprised. I felt bad about the miscarriage, but not about how she screwed him over. At the end of the message, he asked if I would be a witness in the court proceedings. I took a few days to think about it and then agreed.

Out of curiosity I began to research her and her history. It turns out that she had a history of claiming pregnancy and then extorting men for money when she either 'got an abortion' or 'miscarried'. She somehow got pregnant and miscarried 11 babies in one year, and she was screwing over women who sympathetically took her in based on her sob story.

He and I both realized that we had been swindled and decided to join forces to make sure she didn't do it again. This was harder than we thought because she had an excuse for every missed court date and then she went off grid.

I cut her off and blocked her from everything. She had taken up too much of my time, money, and energy and I wasn't about to spend anything else on her. Once the dust settled, I realized how poor my mental health was and that I was using her drama to escape my own pain.

By May, I was broke and suicidal, it was clear that I needed to work on my mental health. My lease was running up at the beginning of June, and I decided to move back home in order to save some money and commit to therapy.

Jennifer was traveling for work more often than not and I was working on my blog and on therapy. Despite my efforts to stay above water, I was sinking deeper and deeper into despair. It got to the point where I was suicidal every night and decided I was either going to go to treatment, or I was going to end my life.

Being on Medicare severely limited my options for treatment. After a few days of feverishly searching for a facility that would take my insurance, I finally found an 'institution' masked as a trauma treatment clinic and decided that was the one. As I packed to get ready to leave, I was aware that this was the bottom, that any further down, I would be dead. The flashbacks, nightmares, night terrors, repetitive inner dialogue, and suicidality was all too much.

As I walked to the security checkpoint at the airport, I got a call… from Stephanie. *Exactly what I need…* I tried to mask my irritation,

"Hello?"

"Oh my God, Hailey! How are you doing? I saw you were going to go to treatment and worried!"

She was so bad at faking sympathy.

"Yes, I'm in the airport right now so I can't really talk." I began to hang up.

"Wait, so I've really been struggling lately and wanted to know if you have any suggestions for a therapist?"

Insert eyeroll… "Stephanie, this really isn't a good time, I'm in a dark place and I'm doing everything I can to get to treatment alive."

Silence.

"Oh, yeah, okay, well just text me when you get back."

"Okay…" I lied.

I got to my gate, checked in, sat by the window and wept. I didn't know how I was going to last the next twelve hours. I picked up the phone and called my boyfriend. We had been together for about a month and he was very supportive of my decision to go to treatment. He offered for me to read his coveted and hardly shared novel so I could distract on the plane. He emailed it to me and I devoured it, every character felt familiar as it was based on him and his friends in a barber shop. Having been a hairstylist, it was a comfort.

I arrived in Dallas and got a taxi to the clinic. It was dark out and I was overwhelmed. The driver and I sat in silence as he drove. I looked out the window as the Dallas skyline began to get smaller. After a good half hour, the taxi pulled up to a large dimly lit hospital. He pulled in to the long drive, ending up at a small house that stood as the 'front office'. I stepped into the building with my suitcase and terror coursing through my body. I looked back and the taxi drove away. There was no turning back now.

It was 10pm when I walked up to the plate glass window where a tired middle-aged woman was working. She looked up from her computer,

"Can I help you?"

They should've known that I was coming; I had been speaking to them over the last 3 days, planning my arrival and admission.

"I, um, I'm here for the trauma clinic. I have been working with Sharon on my admit."

She looked plainly at me, "Do you have a photo id and insurance card?"

I scrambled through my purse, handed them to her.

"Okay, go ahead and have a seat, I'll be with you in a bit."

I walked over to a couch with ripped faux leather cushions, sat down and surveyed the room. A broken tiled floor supported another couch and a coffee table and led to a fireplace that hadn't been used since this office was actually a house. An hour passed, I leaned over with my elbow on the arm of the couch, rested my cheek on my palm and fell asleep.

Sometime later, I was startled awake by something. I looked at my phone, it was 11:30pm and my arm was asleep. Whatever woke me up had also rustled up the cockroaches that lived between the bricks on the fireplace. They scurried back and forth for another half hour until the lady behind the plate glass called out,

"HAILEY?" She yelled like there were a lot of people in the room. It was just me.

I got up and followed her down a hall to a makeshift interview room. She sat me across from a computer screen.

"The psychiatrist will be right with you, we had to wake him up because you came in so late."

Embarrassed, I sat for a few minutes before the screen turned on and there was a very tired and grumpy psychiatrist staring at me.

"Why are you here?"

"I'm suicidal."

"Are you homicidal?"

"No."

"Do you hear or see things that aren't there?"

"No."

"Is suicidality your only symptom?"

Isn't that enough?

"No, I have a long history of trauma that is causing incessant flashbacks and insufferable nightmares."

"Okay, sounds good, I signed your papers, go sit in the waiting room and they will take you to your room."

Welcome to the Shit Show

Age 30

Another hour passed. I was lost in thoughts, the same familiar "I hate my life, I hate my life, I hate my life" pulsed through my brain. The only distraction were the cockroaches who I'd become accustomed to. *I wonder if they have names?*

The lady abruptly came back into focus. "HAILEY?"

Jesus Christ, I'm the only one here!

I stood up and followed her outside, down a long sidewalk which arrived at the side door of the hospital. I looked up and it towered over me like a medieval castle, black and daunting. She was silent. I followed her up 3 flights of stairs which emptied out into a small hallway. We walked to the end of the hallway where a nurse's station sat – again, behind plate glass.

"Here she is." The woman told the nurse and walked away leaving me to navigate their confused stares.

"Did you tell anyone you were coming?"

My social anxiety was at its max and I felt my face begin to droop. "Yes, I have been working with Sharon in admissions for 3 days, she told me you would be expecting me."

The nurses rolled their eyes. "Hold on, I'll be right back."

I stood like a lost puppy for at least ten minutes. To my right was a door that said "TRAUMA UNIT" and to my left was a door that said "GERIATRIC

UNIT". After what seemed like forever, the door to the geriatric unit opened and two short Hispanic women ushered me in.

Wait, wait, this is the wrong unit. I screamed inside but couldn't get the words out. I followed them silently to a communal bathroom. One of the women didn't speak English at all, and the other in broken English told me to strip.

What the FUCK is this?? I couldn't speak, but tears started to stream down my cheeks. I could see that they felt my pain in their eyes. The woman who could only communicate with her eyes went to get a nurse.

"Is everything okay here?" A nurse around my age stepped into the bathroom with us.

"Wh…Why…" I couldn't say anything more.

She explained that a strip search is required of every patient so they knew we weren't bringing in anything that could hurt ourselves or others. My tears turned into rivers down my cheeks.

I slowly pulled my t-shirt over my head, and sheepishly unbuttoned my pants. The head rush of flashbacks overwhelmed me. The familiar ice filled my veins, everything went silent, and a stoicism overtook me. I straightened my spine and complied with their orders. Once fully naked, they lifted my breasts to see that there was nothing under them, they motioned for me to turn around toward the wall, to squat, and then to cough. I could tell that this was just as traumatic for them as it was for me.

Once I was deemed to have no contraband, they motioned for me to dress again and then brought me to a small room in the geriatric ward. Confused I begged them to get the nurse.

The nurse came to my room, "Did you need something?"

I was curled up in the corner of the stark cement cell with the sheet and cardboard pillow they had provided. "Um, yes, I need my night meds and I think I'm in the wrong ward."

She looked irritated, "Well, you showed up in the middle of the night and we don't have a bed for you in the trauma unit just yet. You will have to wait for the psychiatrist to come in before we can order your meds." She turned and locked the door on the way out. I felt like a prisoner.

Between the screaming patients, the random thumps and shuffles, the cold room, and the profanity etched windows, I was only able to sleep for an hour or two before the sun began to rise. *Once I see the psychiatrist, I'm discharging, this is not okay.* I was determined to save myself from this hell hole before it got worse.

Once the sun was pouring into my room, a nurse came to my room and apologized for the miscommunication the night before. "I spoke to Sharon, and we didn't realize you were slated to come last night, we thought you were coming tonight."

I began to sob, grateful for meaningful human contact with someone who actually cared how I felt. She came over to me, helped me to my feet and ushered my exhausted body out of the geriatric ward and into the trauma ward.

ANNIKA ROSE

The Diagnosis

Age 30

It was like a different world. The patients were dressed normally, the lights were bright, and the nurses seemed to care that I was there. There was a softness to the ward that was sorely lacking on the geriatric side. The patient rooms lined the four exterior walls. In the middle was the day room where a few patients were gathered playing a board game.

A woman in plain clothes came up to me and introduced herself as the head patient for the day. She showed me to a warm room with a single sized bed, a small desk, and a locked bathroom. On the head of the bed was one sheet, one wool blanket, one pillow, and one pillowcase. At the foot of the bed were the items deemed 'safe' from my suitcase. She explained that we are not allowed to have any more than that.

I made my bed and put my items in the under-bed drawers, then curled up and fell asleep.

"Hailey?" a knock on the open door, "Hailey, are you awake?"

I blinked slowly, feeling exhausted, "Yes."

A short nurse came in, "Are you feeling settled in at all? I know it can take a while."

After the last 24 hours, I was empty of will, of thoughts, of hope. I hadn't had any of my meds since 8am the morning before.

"Do you know when I will get my meds? I'm starting to feel sick and I either want to die or go home." My exhausted frenetic energy vibrated off my body and charged the room. I shook uncontrollably.

"The psychiatrist will be here later this afternoon and he will do your intake at that time."

I don't know if I can make it until then. I began to panic.

She sat next to me and rubbed my back as I sat dejected on the edge of the bed.

"I know this is hard, but you made the right decision. You are in the right place."

Her compassion was the key that unlocked the floodgates of my emotions.

I began to sob, "I don't know what to do, last night was so scary and I can't stop having flashbacks, and I feel so out of place, and I just want to go home, and I think I'm going to spontaneously combust if I don't escape."

She listened patiently. "Are you wanting to harm yourself or anyone else?"

Yes, YES I do, I want to die. "I just wish I could disappear and that the pain would end."

She nodded, "I understand. Would you like to nap for a while until the psychiatrist gets here?"

"Yes, please, I would like that."

An hour later that same nurse came to wake me up. "Hailey, the doctor is ready to see you."

Finally, I'll get my meds. I walked across the day room to his office, fully aware of the other patients' curious gaze.

"Hailey?"

"Yes."

"Can you tell me a bit about why you are here?"

"I can't, I'm so sick, my head is spinning, and I need my meds, I haven't had them in almost 18 hours."

"We can get that remedied, but first I need to see what is going on."

"Please, either let me go home or just overdose me or something, I can't do this anymore." I was desperate.

I filled out a few questionnaires as he watched on. When I was done, there was a verbal questionnaire.

"Do you seem to 'lose' time? Like do you have times in the day that you can't account for?"

"Yes."

"Do you ever end up places, confused as to how you got there?"

"Yes."

"Has anyone ever come up to you that you didn't know that seemed to know you?"

"Yes."

How does he know this stuff? I've never told anyone about that.

"Do you ever have internal dialogue that you don't have control over?"

"Like a committee? Yes."

"Have you ever felt like you were watching yourself do things but you were not in control of the words you were saying or what your body was doing?"

"Yes."

This is creepy, what the actual fuck?

"I understand that you are struggling. I'm going to have you see the therapist for the rest of your intake. He will see you in about an hour, and then he and I will get together to create a treatment plan."

The conversation was done, he opened a different file and asked me to get the next patient.

I went to the nurse's station and asked if I could make a call.

"The phone is only available from 7pm to 9pm and there are only two."

It was only 4pm. I took a risk and sat in the day room with my journal and began to write about my experience. Shortly after I sat down, a short rotund man with a kind face came out and introduced himself as my therapist.

We entered his dimly lit office. I chose the big plush chair in the corner and curled up as tight as I could with my legs on the seat. He asked me about the last couple of months, and then he asked the same questions that the psychiatrist had asked, and I answered the same way I did to the psychiatrist.

"Hailey, have you ever heard of Dissociative Identity Disorder?"

"Yes, but I don't know anything about it."

"Well, it used to be called multiple personality disorder."

"Okay…" My stomach sank.

"Well, I spoke with the doctor and we agree that you have multiple identities that you are likely unaware of."

Tears streamed down my face. I was devastated. I was certain I was now deemed crazy, psycho, untouchable, unlovable. I had no words.

Over the next few days, I learned that DID is caused by severe, prolonged, inescapable childhood trauma, and that I was one of 4 people in the unit that had it. The other three had gotten used to their diagnosis, but I was still grappling with it.

I saw the therapist every other day for an hour and a half, during which, he was able to trigger different parts of my system to come out and speak with him. Apparently, those other parts of my psyche had an inkling that they were alters. I was the last to know.

Everything began to make sense. The committee meetings in my head, the other person repeating "I hate my life", people accusing me of doing things I knew I didn't do, people knowing me that I didn't know… it was all fitting together.

Taking Off the Blinders

Age 30

Each day became the same thing, wake up, do hygiene, have breakfast, do groups, have lunch, attend therapy and/or doctor appointments, free time to work on therapy assignments, dinner, phone time, and then bed.

The most taxing assignments were very personal to me. In the first of two major assignments, I wrote a detailed, minute by minute account of what would happen from the moment I took my life through the next 3 days. Who would find me? Who would call 911? Who would handle my funeral and burial out of my 3 parents? Who would be irreparably harmed by my decision?

This assignment broke my heart because I knew it would be my brother that would find me, and I just couldn't do that to him. I made a vow that as long as I had a flicker of light in my heart, I would stay alive.

The second was to write a timeline of my trauma. What was the year? Who was the perpetrator? What was the offense? Did anyone try to protect me?

Every time I worked on this one, I fell asleep. Pen to paper, lights out. It was the conversion disorder protecting my brain, but I continued to try, day, after day, after day. I finally finished it 23 days into my stay, the day I was discharged.

When I was recapping what I had learned on the last day, I realized that I had become well versed in the DID lingo. "System" was the whole group of alters, "Alter" was one part of the system, "Dissociative Amnesia" was the memory loss that happened to me when other alters were present, and "Integration" was when all the parts become one after a long time of therapy.

I was now aware of eight alters in my system. I was starting to face what I had gone through - recognizing that none of it was normal. I told my mom and sister about the diagnosis, and to my surprise, they said everything made sense to them. The only person I didn't have the courage to tell was my boyfriend. I knew it would be too much and it would scare him off.

11:00am was discharge time. I gave hugs to all the patients that became my friends, this group of survivors helped me get through the 23 days and were integral in my acceptance of the diagnosis.

I was escorted from the unit back to the sad house that sat in front of the hospital. The lady at the desk gave me back my phone (which I hadn't been in possession of since the day that I arrived). The taxi arrived and I said goodbye to the hospital that both traumatized me and helped me begin to heal.

I stepped into the taxi and turned the phone on. I was flooded with texts, voicemails, social media notifications, and emails. I turned it back off and threw it in my purse. I was raw, unprotected, and terrified of the next steps. I kept reminding myself *I've been through worse; I can get through this.* The committee agreed and supported me along my journey back home.

Moving Forward

Age 30

My sister Savannah greeted me at the airport and took me right to the pharmacy where we filled the prescriptions I was given by the psychiatrist. Alex, my eight-year-old part, came out and sheepishly showed the toy cars that she found on an endcap to my sister. To my surprise, Savannah took very well to my younger parts, even though she didn't understand the disorder.

To be fair, neither of us understood the disorder. Even though the DID was born in my early childhood, I was now aware of my alters and through treatment, the alters became cautiously comfortable with coming out. We were in uncharted territory.

I sent text after text to my boyfriend, each one unanswered. I was confused because we spoke every night while I was in treatment.

I sent a final text, "If you found someone else, I understand, just let me know please so I'm not sitting here waiting for you like a fool."

He responded, "No, I didn't find anyone else, I found out that I have a daughter that was just born and have been devoting time to her. I was afraid to tell you because I didn't want to overwhelm you."

Well, that changes things… "Wow, that is exciting! I get it. Just give me a heads up when you want to get together. I missed you."

Silence.

The ghosting went on for two weeks, and at that point, I figured he had moved on. On a whim, I opened my dating app and saw that I had a few messages. One was from a guy that was a writer for a Christian magazine. He and I began to talk in the app and found that we were both passionate about writing, about our faith, and he seemed to be everything that I was looking for on paper.

Our first date was at a park. I pulled up to a beautifully manicured park, carpeted with green grass and adorned with weeping willow trees in full bloom. I stepped out of my car and felt the warm sun on my face. I missed that feeling when I was in treatment. I walked over to a picnic bench where Glenn was waiting. He got up and gave me a hug that emitted the compassion and empathy that I had been missing in the last few weeks.

We sat on the same side of the table and talked, and talked, and talked. Before we knew it, an hour and a half had passed and the fact that we had so much in common did not escape me. The more we conversed, the closer I felt to him. As a bonus, he was just as passionate as I was, and the chemistry was intoxicating. We tried to say goodbye multiple times, each time starting another branch of conversation.

Finally, the sun began to go down and a chill filled the air. He noticed that I was cold and walked me to my car. He hugged me with the warmth of the sun and then kissed me. When I say he kissed me... he *kissed* me. Everything in me lit up and I melted into his arms. After a minute or so, I became aware of a family that was playing at the playground and immediately got self-conscious.

"Glenn... Glenn, there are people watching."

He kissed me one more time and tucked me into my car.

He said he lived right down the street, so he was going to walk. He disappeared down the road as I sat in my car with a stupid cheesy smile, just basking in the energy that was exchanged in the few hours we spent together. I couldn't wait to see him again, and apparently neither could he, because we met again a few days later.

Same Song, Different Verse

Age 30

I drove up to his apartment complex around 3:00pm. He met me at the door, kissed me with the same passion he had at the park, and then ushered me to his home. His kids were watching a movie, which startled me. I couldn't believe I was meeting his kids on the second date.

He had shared that he was recently divorced. "My ex is supposed to pick up the kids any time now, and then we can be alone."

I was still in shock that his kids were in this two-bedroom apartment, with me, a complete stranger.

"What time will she be here?" I wasn't irritated, just uncomfortable, even though the kids weren't fazed by my presence.

Unbothered, he answered, "She's supposed to be here at 3:30."

I sat with the kids and watched whatever cartoon they were watching, excitedly exchanging glances with Glenn, who was across the room. After a half hour or so, he got a text that his ex-wife was outside waiting for the kids. I made the executive decision to stay in the apartment. I had no idea what kind of dynamic there was between them, and the last thing I needed was to cause her to fly off the handle.

He entered the apartment, made a bee-line for me, and kissed me. "Do you want a tour of the apartment?" He grabbed my hand.

"Of course." I smiled with blushed cheeks.

From the living room, we walked through a doorway into the kitchen.

"This is where the cooking happens"

I flirted, "Oh are you a good cook?"

"I guess you'll just have to find out."

The cheeky banter continued as he showed me the kid's bedroom where there were bunk beds covered with stuffed animals and character printed comforters.

He led me to the other side of the hallway, into the doorway of his bedroom.

"I just have to change my shirt before we go anywhere"

I lingered in the doorway.

"You can come in and sit down if you want, I don't bite."

I giggled and sat cross legged on his bed and exhaustion set in.

He smiled lovingly, "You look like you need a nap."

I smiled, "I mean, you're not wrong."

He shared how his car had broken down, but that he had a meeting to go to for the magazine at 7:00pm.

"I'm not sure how I'm going to get there, but I need to go... I guess I'll figure it out."

"Oh no, I can take you, it's on my way home anyway." I was eager to help.

"No, I couldn't ask you to do that."

"No, really, I'd be happy to."

We both laid down, agreeing to take a quick nap before we did anything else. He began to kiss me, which I welcomed. Nothing like a good 'ole teenage make out session. It felt super innocent, and I felt so safe in his arms. The rose-colored glasses were blinding.

His hand traveled down to my butt. He grabbed a hand full and pulled me close. A red flag shot up in my head, four or five alters screamed "DANGER". I ignored them, intoxicated by the physical safety I felt in that moment. Our fingers entwined; he pulled my hand down...

"No, I do not want to do anything today. Kissing only, okay?"

"Yeah, okay, totally." He let my hand go and embraced me.

"You are safe with me." I relaxed my body.

We kissed for a few more minutes until he grabbed my hand and guided it to his crotch again.

"Glenn, I said I don't want to do anything else today." My voice was firm, surprising both of us.

"Sorry, I just want to show you how you make me feel. You are irresistible."

I blushed, "Thank you for that, but I'm really just not comfortable with any other physicality other than kissing."

He softened and kissed me on the forehead. "Why don't we try to nap?"

"Yeah, I'm exhausted."

I turned over and he spooned me, right arm under my neck, and left arm wrapped over my waist.

He whispered, "You are beautiful."

I sighed and drifted into a dreamy state of relaxation. Just as I was falling asleep, I felt his hand navigating the waist of my yoga pants. Like a ninja, I grabbed his hand, turned my face to him,

"Knock it off. One more time and I'm leaving." Why I gave him so many chances, I'll never know.

All of the sudden, in one move, he flipped me onto my back, pulled my yoga pants down to my ankles and slipped into me. I froze.

"What are you doing? I said NO."

"Just take it, you'll like it, just relax."

He pulled my shirt up over my head but stopped at my elbows and then pinned my arms to the bed. Heavily breathing into my face as he violated me, he began to repeat,

"Tell me who owns you. Tell me who owns that pussy."

I turned my head to the right and escaped into his closet in my mind. He roughly turned my chin back to him,

"Tell me."

If I fight, I'm going to get hurt even more. Just do what he wants, get him off as fast as possible.

In a plain voice, I heard myself say "You do, you own me."

"That's right, I do."

Shortly after that admission, he pulled out, came on my stomach, got up, threw a shirt at me and said "Clean up I have to get to my appointment."

I was numb. I pulled my shirt back down, cleaned up my stomach, pulled up my pants, and stood up. I didn't own my body; I was a floating ghost. Somehow, we made it to my car. The ride was silent. When we pulled up, he tried to kiss me. I recoiled and looked out the window.

"What's wrong? We had fun. I'll call you after my meeting."

I pulled out of the parking lot slowly and called my sister.

"How was the date?" She asked brightly.

Another alter, I'm unsure who, came out and said, "Whelp, we did it, apparently I don't have any self-control."

She chuckled and started talking about something benign and unremarkable.

"Uh-huh… yep… yeah, I hear that." I tried to keep up.

A New Response

Age 30

A half hour later, I arrived at home. I went to the couch and smothered myself in a blanket and pulled my computer out. I typed "What constitutes sexual assault?" Google quickly populated a response:

REACH OUT TO SOMEONE TODAY

RAINN | The nation's largest anti-sexual violence organization.

Call 800-656-HOPE to speak with someone today.

I took a deep breath and dialed the numbers on the screen.

"Hello, this is Amber, how can I help you today?"

"Um… I think I've maybe been assaulted, but I'm not sure, because I put myself in the position, and I didn't leave when I said no the first time, and then I stayed even though I said no 4 or 5 times, I can't really remember, but it's probably not assault, I'm sorry, I didn't mean to waste your time." I went to hang up the phone.

"I hear you. Can I ask who I'm speaking to?" Her voice was calm and kind.

I was surprised, "Um, um, my name is Hailey."

She continued, "Okay Hailey, thank you for reaching out today, I know that it is really hard to talk to anyone when you are unsure. Can you take a deep breath for me?"

I filled my lungs and released, "Yeah, I did."

"Okay, so I want you to know that you can give or take away consent at any time with any person, regardless of how far you have gone. It is never your fault if someone did not listen to your boundaries."

"Okay." I didn't have any other words.

"From this end of the phone, it sounds like your boundaries were violated, does that sound right?"

"Um, yeah, I told him to stop, and he didn't."

"Okay, that sounds like it was sexual assault. I'm so sorry that happened to you. You did not deserve that."

I began to tear up, "What now?"

"From here you get to make the choices, the power is in your hands, okay? You can choose to go to have an assault assessment done at the hospital where they will have a nurse that specializes in assault victims. If you choose to do that, they will give you the option of reporting the incident to the police, which is also completely your choice. You do not have to do anything you don't want to."

"I'm afraid that I am being a drama queen. What if it wasn't that bad and I'm just remembering it as really bad?" My hands were trembling, terrified of getting in trouble for telling the truth.

"Like I said, any breach of your boundaries is not okay, and you have the choice to stay home and protect yourself, or to go to the hospital and have the kit done. Neither is better or worse, it is all up to you."

This was the first time in my life that I was walked through what to do after an assault, and that I was not shamed for 'putting myself in a bad situation', or 'asking for it', or 'leading someone on'. She was so kind, and it meant the world to me that she was giving me the options, empowering me and empathizing at the same time.

"Okay, I'm going to think about it for a few minutes."

"Okay Hailey, we are here 24/7 if you need to call back, about anything, we are here for you."

We hung up the phone. My mind swam with options, consequences, doubt, confusion, and fear. I called my brother up from downstairs. I told him what happened and asked if he could please drive me to the ER that was a town away.

"I'm so sorry, I'm not sober and shouldn't be driving, did you ask Savannah?"

"No, not yet."

"I'm really sorry sis. I love you though."

"I know, thank you."

Through tears, I called my sister back, "I think I was assaulted, and I need to go to the ER, can you please take me? I don't think I can drive right now."

I could sense her hesitance. "I'm confused, we just talked, and you said you didn't have self-control, how is it assault now?"

I cried harder, "I told him no, and thought it was my fault because I didn't leave, but the people at the assault hotline talked me through it. I really just need to go to the hospital. Can you please take me?"

"I mean, I guess, give me like 10 minutes and I'll come pick you up."

ANNIKA ROSE

The Exam

Age 30

About 10 minutes later, I was lowering myself into her car, "I am so sorry, thank you for doing this, I know it's taking away from your date night. I'm really sorry."

She was quiet.

We drove to the hospital as I switched alters rapidly. The law stated that they weren't supposed to take my information, and they were just supposed to treat me, but the intake woman asked for my insurance anyway. I didn't have the wherewithal to fight with her. Feeling like a complete burden, I walked with the nurse through the double doors, past a nurse's station, and into a corner room.

"What brought you in today?"

Sheepishly I responded, "I was assaulted and need to see someone about it. I don't know what happens now…"

"Okay, well we will have to call the SANE nurse who handles these situations. She's on call, so we need to get her to come in to the hospital. Let me work on getting her for you."

We sat in the small room for three hours before they came in and said they could not get ahold of a nurse, and that they couldn't accommodate my situation at such a small hospital. They suggested we drive closer to the next major city to get help.

Dejected, I walked to the front door, my sister following behind me, texting rapidly.

We got into the car, and I suggested a different hospital, one that I had been to for eating disorder treatment. She started to drive.

Thirty minutes later, she dropped me off in the emergency room bay and went to park the vehicle. I went in and explained the situation, and the nurse quickly took me back to a room, bypassing intake. They seemed to know what they were doing.

After an hour, the SANE nurse arrived. She was disheveled, but at least she was there.

"Can you tell me what happened dear?"

I went through the whole story, including how I questioned if it was assault. "I mean, if it wasn't assault, I can go… I don't mean to waste anyone's time."

She was warm, "No, Hailey, you went through something traumatic tonight, and it is natural to question if what you went through was your fault, but I can assure you, it was not."

My sister softened with the assessment that the nurse gave. She reached out and held my hand for the rest of the exam.

The next half hour was horrendous. Swabs, pictures, charting, giving up my clothes, being handed a bag of donated clothing gathered specifically for women who had been assaulted. I cried through the whole process.

"Okay, Hailey, you did so good, I am so sorry that this is so hard. You have the choice of whether or not to report this to the police, it is totally your decision though, you don't have to."

My head was swimming, it was three in the morning, and I was exhausted. "Yes, I think I will."

This will have been the first time that I reported any of my abusers. The fear of being called a drama queen, or being accused of faking it, or anyone suggesting that I asked for it was paralyzing. She asked what county the assault happened in. I told her. She made a call and came back 10 minutes later.

"Okay, an officer will reach out to you tomorrow to take your statement."

To Protect and To Serve

Age 30

We drove home, both exhausted. I was so dissociated that I think I just rolled out of the car and went to bed, the memory is fuzzy.

The next day, a detective called me and invited me to go into the station to give my statement. Hesitantly, I did. I told the detective everything that had happened, that I had gotten a rape kit done, and that they took my clothes at the hospital. I gave her all of Glenn's information, his address, and his social media account. She thanked me for my time and said she would be in touch.

Two days later, she called me back and I went in to meet her.

"Okay, so the good news is that we found him to be a con artist. He duped you by appealing to your faith and your love of writing – he found all of that on your social media, as did we."

How is that good news? "Okay…"

She continued, "We had an officer go out to talk to him."

My blood ran cold and I got dizzy, "How did that go?"

"Well, he said that it was all consensual, and that it was a second date. He said he thought everything went well, so this was a surprise to him."

Tears welled in my eyes.

"That doesn't mean that you are lying. Predators often stalk their victims and appeal to their passions and insecurities. He is definitely a predator."

I sensed where this was going.

"Let me just clarify again: You didn't hit him, scratch him, or leave any bruises on him, correct?"

"That's correct, I froze."

"Okay, and he didn't hit you, scratch you, or leave any bruises on you, correct?"

"Yes, that's correct. He didn't cause any damage because, quite frankly, he has a small dick." My anger started to rise.

"Okay, so I hear what you are saying. Unfortunately, the district attorney's office doesn't feel that this case is very strong due to the muddy nature of it. He says it was consensual, there are no signs of resistance… it's just going to be hard to prosecute."

"So, what does that mean?"

"We aren't saying it didn't happen, but the DA's office is declining to press charges at this time."

My blood ran cold, I gathered my things, looked at her plainly, asked if there was anything else she needed, and walked out of the station. I vowed to myself that if I was ever raped again, no one would know about it.

Healed?

Age 30

Halloween night I was at home paralyzed with fear of tiny humans with masks knocking on the door, startling me, and then expecting a certain amount of candy from me.

I called my mom, "Hey, I'm paralyzed, and I'm contracting for safety because I'm having suicidal thoughts and want to be accountable."

She was used to this conversation now. "Okay, so, what about going to the prayer night that you had talked about at that new church? That would be something to take your mind off of everything and feel safe for a while?"

I was undecided, but as the time to leave approached, I began to get ready. I put on a sweatshirt and yoga pants and headed out.

At around 8:00pm, I drove up to a massive structure with an enormous cross sprouting out of the top. There were a handful of cars in the parking lot, mostly luxury SUVs. I parked my modest grand am and walked apprehensively to the long line of double doors. Taking a deep breath, I walked through to find a huge great room that lead to an even larger sanctuary.

No one was there.

I began to wander around, my heart beating out of my chest. *How is this any better than being at home?* Contemporary Christian music started to become louder as I approached a second sanctuary. My entry gained the attention of 4 women casually chatting. On the left were two older ladies, likely in their 60's, one tall and lanky, and one short and petite. On the right were two middle aged women, one with blonde hair and fair skin, and one with brown hair and more of an olive complexion.

"Hello! How can we help you? Are you here for the prayer night?" The brunette woman could barely keep her enthusiasm in.

I need to go, I should go, this is too personal. "Is this it?" I said sheepishly.

The blonde woman chimed in, "Yes, come on over, have a seat!"

I sat with my foot under me and my sweatshirt bunched in front of my stomach, feeling far too exposed.

The group started asking questions, "So… tell us about you." "What brought you in tonight?" "Do you need prayer?"

It was all overwhelming, "No, I just thought we were praying for other people tonight, and I was coming to do that because Halloween is a hard night to be alone." *Too much information, why did you give them that much information?*

The next twenty minutes was a barrage of prodding and poking at what may be wrong with me and how 'The Lord' could set me free.

I don't know how they coaxed it out of me, but eventually I was telling my story, "I came tonight because I was at home, suicidal. I have complex PTSD, and was just diagnosed with Dissociative Identity Disorder…"

Before I could finish, I noticed their plain sympathetic looks, like deer in the headlights. Their reaction gave away their lack of knowledge of DID.

"Basically, I have multiple personalities. It happens from bad child abuse, and I'm feeling so lost…" *Jesus, Hailey, recover, turn back, too much!* "…but I know it wasn't my fault, and I just have a very flexible brain, and yeah… I should go."

I started to get up, reaching down to my left to get my purse, and I felt a hand on my right shoulder. I shuttered. Above me was the blonde woman looking down at me like I was a shelter dog that needed to be saved.

"Wait, don't go, you have a possession over you and you deserve to be free, that's what we are here for tonight. That is why the Holy Spirit brought us here for. You do not have any disorders; you have attachments that need to be removed."

My face was on fire, not from embarrassment, but from anger.

FIRST of all, do not put your hands on me, especially when I am not expecting it. SECOND… Who do you think you are to call me possessed and to basically say that my trauma didn't happen, and my parts aren't my parts?? Do your research on mental health and then we can talk.

I hid my internal rant, "I'm not sure about that. People have mental illness, that's just part of life."

The brunette lady, waiting patiently to speak, came over and put her hand on my left shoulder, and softly spoke, "That's what the enemy has told us in this earth, that it's okay to have disease and illness, but you are meant for more, much more. Please let us pray for you for a few minutes."

I froze, I didn't want to be rude, but I wanted to leave. A part of me wanted to see if I could get any benefit from being prayed for, and another part of me felt like we would be denying that Jesus can work miracles… what would leaving say about my faith?

The two older women slowly walked over and stood behind me, their hands on my back. I dropped my head and closed my eyes.

It began, three hours of 'healing'.

The woman to my left started in, "Okay Lord Jesus, we come here today, we gather here, because 'where two or more are gathered in your presence, there you are also', you promise that to us Lord and we believe in the promises that you gave to your sons and daughters, for miraculous healings, calling your flock back to your heart, Lord, your heart and your heart only is what we crave Lord, and we are here to pray for this sweet soul here, Lord, fill her up with your Spirit, with your Holy Spirit Lord."

She took a breath, and another woman began to pray, as if there was a spiritual baton being passed.

The tall woman behind me picked up the baton, "We praise you Lord, we *praise* You. Lord, we cast out any demons and principalities that are over your beloved, Lord, In JESUS name we cast out the spirits that are causing this mental health crisis, that make her think there is more than one person in her body, Lord, free her from this bondage…"

The harmony to this overarching melody were the rhythmic repetition of "Yes Lord", and "Amen Lord", and "break all the chains Lord."

As they continued, I started to cry. They 'encouraged' me to name out my trauma so it could be cleansed from my body, so I could be set free. I started, "Molestation", "Brainwashing", "Rape" … each one harder to say than the first. Each one met with "bReAk ThEE ChaINS LORD!"

After an hour or so, they began speaking in tongues, emphasizing every other sentence by pushing down on my shoulders, my back, and my head. My nervous system was so overextended and the now familiar ice flowed through my veins and my mind was clouded. I straightened my spine and felt everything in me lengthen, my body becoming a single pillar, then... silence. The voices went away. The suicidality was gone, and so was any skepticism. They began to jump around. I had been 'healed'!

I was exhausted. We rapped up our conversation, exchanged phone numbers, and they invited me to a Wednesday night prayer group every week. I said I would think about it.

My body felt so light on the way home, so new, so optimistic, so in awe.

Movin on Up

Ages 30-32

I told everyone that would listen about my healing. So much so, that I began to sound like the fundamental evangelicals that I was spending my time with, and I was losing friends and family. Before long, my social circle consisted solely of church friends. It was an echo chamber that villainized any opposing viewpoint. I was in multiple bible studies, going to church 2-3 times per week, and participating in the prayer group that I was initially invited to.

I had been seeing the same therapist for two years until one day I walked in and told her about the 'healing', and shortly after, I decided I was free from the trauma that 'enslaved' me and stopped seeing her. After all, why have a therapist when I had Jesus?

This continued for the majority of 2015 and into 2016 when I started to branch out into online coaching and learning how the universe worked in regards to manifestation and the power of intentions. I began wondering if the God of the universe was big enough to create a world that ran on energy, one that was self-sufficient, one that could have creation and evolution simultaneously.

This was clearly not supported by the fundamentalist evangelical church where creationism and divine healing were concerned. But secretly, I continued to wonder if the healing was in part due to the communal intention of a group toward another being.

At the end of 2016, I went back to working in the salon. Disability payments were not near enough to handle daily expenses, and it was obvious that living with my mom was not working. We get along great when we are living separately, but together, whew, what a mess.

Before long, I moved into my own apartment, changed churches, began making a new circle of friends, and began to date again.

A Destined Companion

Age 33

In the spring of 2017, I was finally feeling settled. The only thing missing was some companionship, so I began to look for a dog.

I was initially looking for a pug because I'd always thought they were cute, but they were expensive and I wasn't finding any at the shelter. I was telling my friend about the lack of availability and he asked if I had heard of "Spots Last Stop", a rescue that was based out of the Twin Cities. I had not.

He opened the website and the first thing I saw was *my* dog. Everything in my soul knew that this was my dog, and this dog was not a pug, rather a black 14-pound chiweenie named Jewel. I do not know why I was so convinced that she was supposed to be with me, but I charged ahead with that as my mindset.

I sat down and immediately filled out the application that was linked under her picture and a half hour later I got a call.

"Hello?"

"Yes, is this Hailey? This is Spots Last Stop calling."

"YES! I mean, yes, it is."

"So, I saw that you applied to adopt Jewel, however there is a family that is doing a home visit tomorrow, so if that falls through, we will call you back."

"Okay, thank you. It will fall through, so I will talk to you tomorrow."

The lady laughed and we ended the call.

The next day after work, I went down to the big box pet store and bought everything for Jewel... I'm talking *everything*, all the way down to her name tag and collar. While I was shopping my phone rang.

"Hello?"

"Hey Hailey, this is Spots Last Stop again. Say, the family that was supposed to see Jewel today fell through because their dogs didn't take to her well."

"I knew it! When can I meet her?"

"Can you come over tonight? She is at the foster's house."

"Absolutely."

I began to drive across town. During the drive I thought about all of the possibilities with Jewel, what her temperament was, and whether she would take to me. The nerves increased as I got closer to the foster family. After a half hour, my little Ford Focus was straining to get up a very steep hill surrounded by dense forest and gated properties. At the top of the hill to the right was the long winding driveway to the foster parent's home.

I drove up and parked the car. As I was getting out, Jewel came bounding down the driveway, jumped right into my arms and snuggled her little snoot into my neck and I began to tear up.

"Hi, I'm obviously Hailey", I introduced myself to the foster mom as she walked toward me.

"Whelp, I see you found Jewel! Or rather, she found you. How do you feel with her, what are your first impressions?"

"Like I told you on the phone, she's my dog. I've known since I saw her face on the website that she would be joining my family."

We both chuckled and walked into the large ranch style home where she invited me to sit at the table while she brought over lemonade and cookies.

"So, tell me about you. What made you want to adopt a dog?"

"I live alone, I was divorced 7 years ago and still suffer from pretty bad PTSD. I guess I want a dog so I have someone to love on and someone to keep me company."

She smiled warmly, "You are fully aware of the responsibilities of a dog owner, correct? Like they need a lot of exercise, regular grooming, vet services, and more."

"Yep, I'm all ready for her, I even bought all the toys and a collar and tag with her name on it."

170

"Oh, what are you naming her?"

"Um, Jewel... isn't that her name?"

"Oh, no, that's just what we named her 2 weeks ago when we got her. We don't know the name she had before because she came from a high kill shelter in Alabama."

"Well, she will be Jewel for now, and then if a different name suits her, I will use that."

We chatted a bit longer, all the while Jewel laid on my lap looking up at me lovingly. We wrapped up and she walked me to my car where I had a spot created on the passenger seat specifically for Jewel.

At first, she didn't want to get in the car, she shook and whined, but after a little coaxing with some treats, she laid down and began to snore softly.

A few weeks had passed, and our routine had become regular. She knew that I was the dispenser of food and treats, and I knew that she now owned my queen-sized bed. I continued to call her "puppy" and "baby", and one day, I called her "Bubbies", and that has been her name ever since.

ANNIKA ROSE

False Advertising

Age 34

A year later, in April of 2018, I had gotten the renewal notice for my apartment and my rent was increasing by $300 per month. I panicked. I begged the apartment to reduce it or to give me a prorated month for free if I signed for another 13 months. My pleas fell on deaf ears.

Frantically, I took to an app for finding roommates and answered a couple of ads for a single room in a single-family home. After vetting 4 or 5 people, I seemed to get along really well with Chloe. She was quite a bit younger than me, but she seemed very mature and I felt comfortable moving Bubbies and I into her home for a 6-month term. I had a bedroom and bathroom to myself, and the utilities were included in my rent, so I was able to save some money.

Before I moved in, I made sure that she was okay using the air conditioning in the summer because I end up in the hospital annually for heat exhaustion, and I wanted to avoid that. She assured me that we could keep the air around 74 degrees which would be a compromise. She also assured me that she didn't smoke in the house, which was an important requirement due to my asthma.

I moved in June 1, 2018 with the expectation that I would be living there until December.

The first few days were great, we got along really well, I settled in to my 9' by 10' room and Bubbies got used to there being a cat around. After about a week, I noticed that Chloe smoked a hookah every night, which made it hard for me to breathe, and caused Bubbies to sneeze incessantly.

I cautiously confronted her, "So, I know that you relax in the evening with your Hookah, I'm just wondering if we can open up windows so that the smoke is not so thick in the house? No offense, I'm just having a hard time breathing and so is Bubbies."

She rolled her eyes, "I mean, sometimes we can, but I don't want bugs to get in the house."

I understood this, however, she had screens, so I don't know why she protested to opening the windows.

Another week went by, and I noticed that the house was getting a lot warmer. I looked at the thermostat and it was regularly set to 81 degrees. Each time I saw that, I reduced it to 74 degrees again, per the agreement that she and I had made.

Chloe was in a particularly bad mood when I came home one night. Under her breath she said, "I guess it's time to freeze my ass off…"

"Excuse me? I missed that."

"Yeah, well I freeze when we have the temp at 74. My bedroom is an ice box, and I'm going to get a cold."

"Well, do you want me to help you close the vent in your bedroom so the air doesn't pour in there while you are sleeping?"

"No."

"Well, you know that I get sick if I get too hot, and 81 degrees in the house with 92% humidity makes it miserable, you know we agreed to 74."

"Yeah, well, I'm not going to get sick in my own house because you are sensitive."

First of all, you don't get sick from being cold. If that was the case, everyone in the northern hemisphere would be sick all the time. Second, you are being a whiney brat. I wanted to say that to her face in the worst way, but as usual, I was 'skillful'.

"I understand that it is a shock, how about we compromise and do 76 degrees?"

"Okay, that works better."

Tah Dah! That wasn't so hard, right? Wrong. The next day I woke up sweating. I stumbled into the hall and immediately swerved into the bathroom to vomit. *How hot is it in here?* After cleaning up, I came out to find that the thermostat was set to 81 again. I wasn't able to fight about it because I was delirious. I looked up the heat index and it was 98 degrees. I was sick, Bubbies was sick, and Chloe couldn't have cared less.

Three hours later, I called Chloe from the ER, "Hey, so I'm in the ER for heat exhaustion. I won't be home until later, can you feed Bubbs?"

"Ugh, fine." I could hear her eyes roll.

I got home, walked straight to the thermostat, turning it down while I looked at her sitting on the couch smoking her hookah. "PLEASE leave it at 76 tonight." I turned around and went to bed with Bubbies.

The next day, I woke up and confronted her before she went to work. "Chloe, we need to talk about whether or not our lease is a great idea. I think it may not be, and we may need to shorten it, drastically."

"Let's talk about it after work." She brushed me off and left the house for the day.

I had had it at this point, and once 5pm hit and we were both home from work, I sat her down and told her that she was not holding up the end of her contract and she can either release me from the contract, or I will report her to the Department of Housing and Urban Development for forcing unlivable conditions.

She agreed, and I was to be out two weeks later, in mid-August.

Fight or flight kicked in and I went to town trying to find an apartment that was in my budget. I finally found one. The neighborhood left some to be desired, but it would be an apartment to myself. No more roommate bullshit.

ANNIKA ROSE

A Sad Reality

Ages 34-35

I moved into the new apartment, in North Minneapolis. On the first night, my best friend came to walk bubbies with me. We wanted to see the area and see where I would be walking every morning and evening moving forward. We began to walk north on the busy road. Trash was strewn along the sides of the pavement and large dogs barked from behind chain link fences. After a block or two, the sun began to fade and we turned back to the apartment.

As we walked up the parking lot entrance, we noticed a commotion by my building. Curious, we walked over, saying hi to the neighbors as we got closer. My stomach dropped and my adrenaline soared. There were 6 sheriff's SUVs surrounding a black sedan with blacked out windows. On the ground, there was a young man, no more than 19 years old, being cuffed and put into the back of one of the squads while other police ripped the car apart. You would think they were looking for a lost toddler... but no, they just had a suspicion of drug activity.

I looked around and the bystanders were not just adults, they were also teens, and their younger siblings. I don't know what I expected, but none of them were surprised, rather, they were taking video of the incident so they would have evidence if something happened to the young man.

Eventually the cops let the young man out of the squad, uncuffed him, and told him they had the wrong guy. He turned around silently, walked to his car, resigning to the fact that this is life, and began to pick up the mess they had made. The police left the complex as quickly as they had arrived.

I looked at the women standing near me, flabbergasted, "Is this normal? I just moved in."

They rolled their eyes, nodded their heads, and walked away.

Nights were loud, fights between partners, children running up and down the halls, and the occasional knock on the door from a police officer, usually looking for someone that did not reside in my apartment.

I worked 40 hours per week at a health insurance company making what should have been good money, but I was barely making rent. I couldn't fathom what it was like for some of these families with three or more children and parents that worked multiple jobs just to stay afloat in a terrible area. The stress must have been unbearable.

Over the weeks and months that followed, I ended up being a friend to the children on our floor. One family in particular had three daughters aged 11, 6, and 3. I had a few conversations with their mom, she seemed nice enough, and didn't mind when they came down to my place while she worked.

It became a nightly event. Mom would leave for work at around 6:00, and I would hear their little feet padding down the hallway to my apartment. We mainly ate popcorn and watched animated movies. Occasionally, I would help the 11-year-old with her homework, and they would walk bubbies with me. I appreciated the company, and they appreciated the safety that my apartment gave them.

For months I didn't know what they were going through until one night when I heard a fight down the hall. When I poked my head into the hall, it was clear that it was coming from their apartment. I texted the 11-year-old,

"Hey, are you okay?"

An uncomfortable 5 minutes went by while insults rang out into the hallway, "You are a little SLUT! You are stupid, you little piece of shit!"

Unfortunately, those types of fights were not rare in my building, but I hadn't heard it come from their apartment, especially after their mom left for work. I hated calling 911 because there was a 50/50 chance that the responding officers would be way less than helpful, but I needed to make sure the kids were safe.

Shortly after I called, I heard the door slam. I looked out to see the boyfriend leaving the building. Simultaneously the 11-year-old peeked out toward my direction. I motioned for her to grab her sisters and run down to me. Moments later, the oldest was holding the hands of the younger two while quickly making their way to my apartment.

Before I could ask what was happening, all three wrapped their little arms around me and shook.

"It's okay. It's okay, you are safe. It's okay."

I walked them to the couch and set them up with blankets and stuffed animals, knowing that the police would be there soon.

KNOCK KNOCK KNOCK

I looked through the peep hole in my door and saw an officer, about my height, but slender. I opened the door just enough to slip out into the hallway.

"So, I don't know exactly what happened yet, but I do know that their mother's new boyfriend was screaming profanities at them, and it seemed to be escalating at the time that I called you."

"Okay, so where are they now? Where is the boyfriend?"

"I think he may have left, but the girls are in my apartment. They come over a lot when their mom isn't home."

I could tell he was trying to piece together why this unrelated woman was harboring three minors.

"I have their mother's permission to have them over, it's just safer while she works."

"Okay, well, I'm going to need to talk to them."

I opened the door and asked the eldest to come out with me, she hesitated.

"I promise it will be okay. You aren't in trouble, and he can't hurt you."

She reluctantly came out into the hallway and curled up into my right arm with her arms around my waist.

He began to ask her for her name and address and her mom's phone number. She whispered it just loud enough for me to hear.

"Honey, you have to tell *him*."

She looked up at me with tears in her eyes.

"Are you scared?"

She nodded her head.

"Officer, is it okay if I tell you what she says? She's scared of police."

He reluctantly agreed and attempted to make himself seem less intimidating. "Can you tell me what happened?"

She whispered to me and I relayed, "She was at home in her bedroom and he didn't like something she was doing so he came in and started yelling at her."

He looked up from writing in his notebook, "Okay, was he physical with you at all?"

"Yes, he punched me in the leg..." She pointed to her mid-thigh. Unannounced tears jumped to my eyes and my face lit on fire as I held her close.

"Okay, was it with a closed fist, or was it with an open hand?"

"Um, I think it was an open hand." She hesitated and looked up at me.

I could feel her fear, "Honey, you aren't in trouble. You can tell him what happened. He's a good cop."

She looked at him for the first time and nodded her head, "Yeah, he had an open hand, and he left to go to work."

He looked at me, both of us silently acknowledging that she initially said he punched her in the leg, and both of us knowing that an open hand in Minnesota is not considered corporal punishment. She was protecting her mother by protecting her boyfriend.

He said he needed to look in both apartments, first mine, and then theirs, to make sure that he was gone and that they were safe. I gave him permission to come into my apartment. Afterward he went down to theirs while I checked in on the little girls. The 6-year-old was still watching the movie while the 3-year-old slept.

I hugged the eldest, "You did so good, I'm so proud of you. It's all going to be okay."

I knew that was a lie, but I didn't know how else to soothe her in that moment.

"Where is your cell phone, we should call your mom and tell her what happened."

She nodded.

The cop spoke to their mother on the phone. She told him it was okay for them to stay with me and that she would be home as soon as she could. He thanked me for watching out for them, we said goodbye, and he disappeared to his next call.

About an hour later, I heard a knock at the door. Again, I peered through the peep hole and saw their mother, looking frantic and exhausted. I opened the door expecting to share a communal sigh of relief, but instead she said sharply, "Where are my kids?"

I was taken aback, "They are right in here, watching a movie, come on in."

"No, I'm fine. Kids, let's go, get back home, now."

They all stood at attention, looked at me as if to say they were sorry, and padded back down the hall to their apartment. Soon after their door closed, I heard her screaming, "DON'T you EVER bring that lady into our business AGAIN!"

I closed my door, brought bubbies to my bed and cried for hours. I didn't know what else I could have done in that situation besides ignore it and let the children be hurt more.

It was a complex situation and I understood that I was not the right person to be a safe haven for her kids, and she made that known. She never spoke to me again, and the kids never came over again. It was eerily silent for a couple of weeks until I asked the old woman who cleaned the halls what had happened. She explained that the mother had a warrant out for her arrest and the kids were taken by social services.

This, among other things, launched me into a relentless depression. It was everything I could do to stay alive and in February of 2019, I decided to get help, again, but this time, it was the fulcrum on which my life pivoted for the better.

ANNIKA ROSE

Every Day Angels

Age 35

Between the nightmares, flashbacks, work drama, home drama, and constantly feeling like I was drowning, I could barely function. I struggled to pay my bills even with a fulltime job and no children. The cost of living in the city had become impossible to keep up with since the wages didn't follow.

Every day was the same thing: Get up, walk Bubbs, go to work, come home, walk bubbs, watch a show, and then go to bed listening to the police scanner to see if they were coming to my floor of the complex that night.

I found myself in the same place that I was in 2014. I was either going to get help, or I was going to take my life.

My dog was the only thing keeping me alive. I couldn't imagine leaving her and having her wonder what happened and if I was coming back.

I started to call around to different residential treatment centers. One after another telling me that they don't take in network insurance which would mean that I had to pay the $9,000 out of network deductible to attend. There's no way I could afford that with the financial hardship I was already facing.

My shift was slow at the call center on a Wednesday night when I made a hail Mary call to Sierra Tucson, a premier treatment center. I was desperate. I spoke to an intake specialist named Sarah. She introduced herself and asked what was going on.

"I'm desperate, I'm suicidal all the time and I have severe trauma that I need to see someone about." Tears began to stream down my face.

She asked me about my history, in great detail. I told her about the rapes, the psychopath ex-husband, the childhood abuse... all of it. She was stunned. I told her that I cannot afford what all the treatment centers wanted me to pay and my next step was just to do an in-network community clinic.

She stopped me in my tracks. "No, absolutely not. You are not going to an in-network clinic that clearly is not made for your level of trauma. Let me make some calls and I'll get right back to you."

I waited on hold for what seemed like an eternity.

She came back on the phone after about 10 minutes. "How much can you afford?"

Defeated, I threw out a number, "I could maybe afford like $200."

Silence on the other end of the line.

"Are you still there Sarah?"

"Yes, sorry, I'm messaging with the clinical director to see what we can do."

A glimmer of hope sprung up in my gut, "Okay..."

A minute passed, "So, like I said, I was talking to my clinical director, and if you can get yourself here, we will cover the rest. We would like to extend a full scholarship."

I sat stunned. *What did she say??*

"Hailey, are you still there?"

I caught my breath, "Yes, yes I am. Are you sure? Am I going to get billed on the back end? How did this happen? Why me?"

Her voice was like a salve, "Hailey, you have been through enough, and the in-network treatment facilities do not have the resources that you need to truly begin to heal. I don't want you to fall through the cracks, and neither does my director."

I agreed and she emailed me the contract, which clearly stated that they would cover everything but my travel expenses and that they would not balance bill the amount that insurance didn't cover. I read every word, making sure I wasn't being set up for another failure. The contract was clear and concise, and I signed it that evening.

The next day, Sarah called me to set up my intake. "Can you be here this Friday?"

It was Wednesday… my mind went into overdrive, *I have to find a place for Bubbies, I have to get leave from work, what if I get fired? Can they fire me for medical? Where is my dog going to go? What about my apartment?*

"Are you still there?"

Startled out of my thoughts, "Yes, I'm just trying to figure out logistics because it's really fast."

We went back and forth for a few minutes trying to troubleshoot my concerns and then decided that it was going to be two weeks before I could make it there. The date was set.

I was going to get help.

After some asking around, I found a co-worker whose friend was willing to take Bubbs for a month. With the state of my depression, along with the fear of going across the country *again* for treatment, I was wrecked over leaving her.

Three days before I left for treatment, I met the family that would be taking care of my baby, I was satisfied that they would be good for Bubbs. We left from meeting the family, went to a local parking lot, and I completely lost it. I hadn't cried so hard since the divorce. My mind spun.

What if she forgets about me? What if she feels like I abandoned her? Does this make me a bad dog mom? What if this family is bad and I just don't know it?

Two nights went by and the morning of the flight had come. I got to the family's house and dropped Bubbs off.

"Okay, don't forget she gets fed twice per day, and needs snuggles in the evening, and I brought Benadryl in case she gets into something or gets too anxious." I was shaking.

"Okay, we've got her, we'll take really good care of her. You go take care of yourself."

"Oh, and here is a document (4 pages long) of everything that she could need and how to handle it."

"Hailey, you are going to miss your flight."

"Okay, I'm going." I hopped into my car and drove away with tears staining my cheeks.

It was in that moment that I realized that by taking care of myself, I was taking care of her. If I didn't go to treatment right now, she wouldn't have a mom for long. I was suicidal every night and the fact that I stayed alive until this point was in large part due to her support and unconditional love.

I wiped the tears from my face and went to the airport.

ANNIKA ROSE

Road Bumps and Relapses

Age 35

I don't remember arriving at the airport or boarding the plane but I do remember the descent into Phoenix where my connecting flight was waiting. My anxiety was mounting. I just had to make it to that next plane, one step at a time.

Right before we landed, I heard a man speaking over the inflight intercom: "Ladies & Gentlemen on your way to Tucson, there has been a mechanical failure on the plane and the flight has been cancelled. Please see the ticket counter to reschedule your flight."

My mind went blank. I looked around and saw faceless passengers moving around, gathering their things, completely oblivious to the internal panic attack that I was experiencing.

I don't know how long I sat there and stared into space, but I came back to reality when a sweet older woman, no taller than the overhead bins spoke kindly to me,

"Honey, are you okay? We have to get off the plane now, do you need help?"

I shook off the cobwebs and kicked into business mode. "Oh good Lord, I'm sorry, I was daydreaming, I guess. Thank you for the kind words but I'm fine." I feigned a smile as best as I could.

With carry on and purse in tow I wobbled off the plane and through the angry crowd that were meant to go to Tucson. I didn't feel the people brushing against me as I pushed through, barely functionally conscious I found a quiet spot and sat for a couple of minutes to determine my next steps.

I pulled out my phone and called Sarah.

"Hey Hailey, how's it going? Are you in Phoenix now? How was your flight?"

"Sarah, my flight to Tucson was cancelled, and I don't know how I'm going to get there, please don't cancel my spot. I don't know what to do next, I'm panicking."

Her soothing voice was reassuring, "Hailey, can you take a deep breath for me?"

My chest expanded and released.

"Okay, we have another patient that was on your flight and is in the same situation. We are working on how to get you here. Don't worry, you will be here by tonight, I promise."

I got my bearings and walked over to the ticket counter. I waited for a half hour for my turn. I walked up to the first computer where a stocky, less than amused woman was looking up at me.

"Can I help you?"

"Yeah, I just got off the Phoenix flight…"

"Yes, I know, were you supposed to be going to Tucson?" Her condescension was jarring.

"Um, yes. I need to get there for treatment. I don't know what to do. I struggle with high stress situations; I just need to know what to do next."

"Well, I don't know what to tell you. You purchased your ticket on a discount site, you need to call them for a reschedule or a refund."

"Wait, you can't get me to Tucson?" Panic seeped into my veins stealing my sense of balance.

"You can buy a new ticket if you want. The next flight is tomorrow." What little patience she had was wearing thin.

I walked away in a daze. *Next steps, what are the next steps?* LUGGAGE. I made my way to the baggage claim. *Once I have my things, I will know what to do.*

Round after round after round I watched the luggage carousel. I checked that I was at the right carousel, yep, Minneapolis to Phoenix. The bags became sparser and I did not see mine anywhere. After a few more rounds, they shut off the carousel and took the few unclaimed bags to the lost and found.

Another wave of overwhelm consumed me. *Next step, what is the next step?*

I went to the lost and found counter. "Um, my luggage wasn't on the carousel from Minneapolis."

A kind man, tall and lanky, asked for my baggage ticket.

He typed quickly, his face a caricature of what he was finding in his system. Finally, he looked at me compassionately, "So, your baggage still went to Tucson. Do you have a flight, or was yours the one that got cancelled?"

Tears welled in my eyes. It was everything I could do not to lose it in front of this stranger who was just trying to help.

"I'm so sorry. Did the airline do anything for you?"

"No, I'll figure it out though." I walked away defeated and dissociated.

I don't know how much time passed, but I came back to reality when my phone rang. I was standing with my nose to a corner, sobbing. I felt so young, I no longer had the critical thinking skills that I had become accustomed to.

"Hello?" a young voice came from my mouth.

"Hailey? Are you doing okay? How are you doing?" Sarah's warm voice was a safety blanket.

The tears began to leap out of my eyes, "No, I went to get my baggage, and it went to Tucson, so I don't have any baggage, nowhere to stay, nowhere to go, I don't know what to do."

"Oh honey, it'll be okay. We have arranged for someone to drive from here to you. Everything is okay. You are safe."

We determined the logistics. The driver would pick me up right outside the door that I was at.

"So, it's a 2-hour drive from the center to the airport, but he will be there. Can you find somewhere to stay safe?" Sarah realized that I needed step by step help at this point. My nervous system was shot.

"Um, yeah."

We hung up and I stood in place, frozen. An elderly woman who was volunteering at the help kiosk came over and lightly put her hand on my arm. She was easily a foot shorter than I was. She stared up at me,

"Dear, are you okay? Can I help you?"

Blankly I stared at her and in a flat voice I heard myself respond, "My phone is going to die."

"Okay, can you come with me?"

We walked 20 feet to the safety of her kiosk. "Do you have a charger for your phone?"

I dug around in my purse and pulled out a charger. "I don't have a block thingy to plug it in though."

She gave a knowing look to the man in the kiosk who pulled out a brick and offered to plug the phone in for me.

This was one of those moments where I wonder if they were really there, or if they were angels sent to help me through an especially difficult time. Their kindness was a balm to my fried nerves.

The next two hours were spent sitting on the floor next to where my phone was plugged in, going in and out of lucidity.

The phone rang, "Hailey? Has he gotten there yet?"

"Um, who is this?" A masculine voice came out of my mouth, I felt miles away from my body.

"Hailey, it's Sarah. Are you hanging in there?"

Again, the masculine voice, "I don't know who you are."

Without missing a beat she picked up the slack, "Okay, can you tell me how old you are?"

"Uh, I think I'm 29?"

"And your name is Hailey?"

"Yeah…"

"Okay, are you seated somewhere safe?"

The voice again, "Yeah, but I have no idea what's going on."

"All you need to know is that we have a driver coming to get you. It will take a couple of hours once you get in the vehicle, but you will be at treatment by tonight. Have you eaten anything?"

"Honestly, I don't know."

It was like a sling shot launched me back into my body, "Sarah? Is that you?"

"Hailey?"

"Yeah, what's going on?" I was genuinely confused.

"The driver is almost there; can you go outside the door and look for a tan suburban? That will be the man that will bring you to the center."

I was compliant, "Yeah, I can. Wait, Sarah, do you think the DID is back?"

190

A pause on her end of the line, "Why don't we talk about it once you get here. It's all going to be okay. You are coming to the right place."

ANNIKA ROSE

Safe and Protected

Age 35

Five hours after my flight landed, we were driving up to a beautiful facility in the foothills of the Catalina mountains. I went through all of the intake information and rules, and they showed me to my bedroom.

It was a large room with 4 twin-sized beds, each fitted with a trunk at the foot where all our belongings were meant to be kept. It was tight, but I wasn't expecting 5-star accommodations. I would have unpacked, but my belongings were still at the Tucson airport. I wouldn't get them back for 2 more days.

I spent most of the first days sleeping. Every time I woke up from a nap, I would panic. *I need to be in a group or something, this is a waste of time, I only get a little bit of time here…* Each time a nurse reassured me that the first days are meant to bring me back to equilibrium, to rest and restore before I started the 'real work'.

I learned that this part of the center was the evaluation section. This is where the nurses and doctors analyzed what each patient was prone to, avert to, and the disorders that they may have, either known, or unknown.

During one of the interviews with the psychiatrist, he commented on my demeanor and presentation.

"You have been through horrific trauma, but you tell me the story with no emotion, like you are reading it from a book."

I felt like I had disappointed him, "Um, I feel like it's someone else' story. I guess I didn't realize that it wasn't normal."

He jotted something down on his pad. "So, I and the treatment team have discussed your case and feel that you have Dissociative Identity Disorder, Complex PTSD, Generalized Anxiety Disorder, and Major Depressive Disorder, all of which exacerbate your long-standing eating disorder."

I sat in silence.

"Does this surprise you? How do you feel about it?" He probed for actual feeling words.

Pulled from the fog I heard myself say, "No, I'm just disappointed about the DID. I thought that was gone."

"Well during your evaluations, we have spoken to three or four of your alters."

"Wait…" the breath was sucked from my lungs, "Am I too much for you to treat? Do I need to go back home?"

Panic took over. The rest of the conversation was muted, as if someone turned down the volume and put cotton balls in my ears.

He eventually ushered me out to the day room and mentioned something in a hushed tone to the charge nurse. She nodded knowingly and smiled at me with reassuring eyes.

Once they decided that I was reliably safe to myself, they began to bring me along with the other patients to groups intended to help us process emotions and begin to work on our trauma.

The more I got out of the initial building, the more I realized how large the treatment center was. It was stunning. The three massive lodges looked over a large inner courtyard which housed a host of native plants cut in with walking paths, all of which led to an in-ground amphitheater in the center. My favorite part of this inner sanctum were the lizards, road runners, and quail that peeked in and out of the cacti and desert grasses. It felt majestic and serene.

After 8 days in the initial lodge, I was deemed ready to go into the general milieu. I was walked with my luggage (that had finally arrived) to the first lodge, the 'Trauma Lodge'. The doors opened and I walked into a massive great room with a nurse's station in the center. To the right was a loft that seemed to be the arts area and underneath was a meeting/tv room. There were offices to the left, and then straight ahead were the patient rooms.

We continued down the patient hall and arrived at my room. I was surprised to find a hotel-like suite with 2 queen sized beds and a large ensuite bathroom. Half of the room was already occupied by an unknown woman with whom I would be sharing this space with. The nurse assured me that my roommate was kind and that I would really like her. I settled in and once again, fell asleep, this time on an incredible mattress that embraced my body like a long-lost friend.

The next 23 days were deep and powerful. On the surface it looked like psychoeducational groups and therapy all day. In reality, it was an exercise in vulnerability, interpersonal relationships, trust, and introspection that brought deep realizations and hope that life could be more than the pain I was in.

I made a commitment to dive in head first, to take all of the lessons and apply them to my life so that I could leave feeling that I had accomplished something.

The most impactful exercise was a journal prompt, "What needs to be different when I go home in order to support my recovery?"

I began to write. The first idea that rolled off the end of my pen surprised me, "I need to move away from Minnesota. I need sunshine and a new start, away from all my triggers." The more I wrote, the more I was sure that I was moving to Tucson, where I felt at home, where the mountains hugged me and turned pink at night.

The last week was family week. Jennifer came down from Minnesota to attend what she thought was a week of touring the campus and hearing about the progress I had made. What really happened was a week of confronting long standing familial issues and creating a plan to move forward in healing.

We made it to the end of the week and decided that it would be better to go back to Minneapolis with her so I have protection and guidance in the airport.

Saying goodbye to my newfound friends was more difficult than I thought it would be. We forged deep connections based on a desire to heal and to do it as a collective. I was scared to leave the comfort and safety that was fostered at the center.

We finished all of our hugs and parting words next to the sedan that Jennifer had rented. As I slipped into the passenger seat, my case manager handed me the bag containing my phone and other electronics and we were on our way.

My first call was to my best friend.

"I'm going to move here." It just came out of my mouth and there was silence on both sides of the line.

"What? I mean, I knew that you were thinking of going somewhere else, but this fast?" The sadness was apparent in her voice.

"Yeah, you know that I don't do well in the winter and all of my triggers are there. I just really need a fresh start and this is the place that feels like home." My tone plead with her to understand.

"Okay, I'll be waiting at the airport for you and we can talk more about it once you get here." Defeated, she ended the call.

A few hours later, Jennifer and I drove into Phoenix where we would stay the night and explore a bit before the flight home.

Big Moves

Age 35

We got home without incident and I went to town packing my apartment. The hardest part was leaving my best friend. I could see the sadness in her eyes and her concern for my safety. I had the longest, most emotional hug with her after we fit all of my belongings into my car like a game of Tetris.

Two weeks later my brother and I drove my overpacked Ford Focus across the country over 3 days to get to my new life. It was an adventure that I will never forget. We spent a night in the black hills so we could see Mt. Rushmore. It was a beautiful day, sunny with a slight breeze. The mountains felt like they were hugging my soul, not unlike the mountains at treatment.

Half way between my old home and new was Denver. I was able to meet up with a friend I had made in treatment. She reminded me that it was the best idea that I was moving to a safer place for my nervous system. She believed in my healing and it was the push I needed to keep driving.

That same day we continued on to Albuquerque, New Mexico where we spent a night in the sketchiest motel I'd ever had the pleasure of inhabiting. The next morning, we were happy to leave and drive the final leg of our adventure. We rolled into my new apartment complex 5 minutes before the leasing office closed – the property manager was not happy to have to work late in order to get me set up, but it was better than having to spend another night in a motel.

I was positive during the whole trip and my switching was pretty minimal. I was still afraid to show any sign of DID to my family, so I masked it a lot.

Once the deposit was paid and I was shown to my new apartment, we unloaded what belongings I had brought and settled in for the night.

I laid down on the air mattress that I had set up in the bedroom and began to sob uncontrollably which launched me into a full-blown panic attack. My brother walked in and just kind of stared at me empathetically, knowing he couldn't do anything to change the come down that I was experiencing.

I kept repeating, "What if this was the worst decision I've ever made?? What if this doesn't work out??".

This decision was so impulsive and I had no idea if I had just created more trauma, or if my life was going to start looking up. I had lived in chaos for years, constantly fearing for my basic needs like financial stability, food security, physical safety, and the need for meaningful connections. I did not realize that while in that state of fear and lack, I was unable to process the trauma that I had experienced.

Moving was terrifying, but turned out to be the best decision I had ever made. Having my brother there for a week also helped tremendously.

Building Safety

Ages 35-36

Once I settled in, I continued with outpatient treatment for both my trauma and my eating disorder. There, I was able to keep the structure that I find so necessary in my life and I met people who were accepting of me as I showed up. This is where I began being more open about having dissociative identity disorder. I was testing the waters with people I didn't really know, but who were also grappling with their own illnesses and disorders. There was no judgement there, and I needed that in order to begin feeling comfortable with how my brain kept me safe for so many years.

Shortly after moving, I began to find safety in my surroundings. I slowly got to know my neighbors and the part of the city I lived in. I went to a few meetup groups in order to connect with like-minded people, despite the crippling agoraphobia that I was experiencing. The friends that I met were outgoing and adventurous. They helped me continue to go out, to dance, try new foods, and become involved in the life energy that surrounded me.

In mid-July, I was running out of time on my short-term disability benefit from my job in Minneapolis. I recused myself from that position and began working at a large car insurance company in the claims department. This move helped me to become financially stable. For the first time in my adult life, I was making more money than my everyday life expenses.

Over time, I developed a routine that helped me attend to my basic needs like eating, sleeping, and maintaining good hygiene. In turn, my system settled a bit and I didn't switch as much in my day-to-day life. While the DID was still very present, I was able to shift from being reactive to being proactive.

Waking Up

Age 36-38

When New Years Eve rolled around, everyone was excited for 2020. It was the beginning of a new decade, a fresh start, and a new adventure. No one knew what was to come and how our world would be flipped on it's head.

I had been in my new job for about 6 months and was excelling at the position. I was building safety in my new home, making new friends, and really enjoying my life. The only hangup was that I was constantly overstimulated at work. The call center that I worked in had fluorescent lights, bright colors, and constant noise. Between the atmosphere, being yelled at on the phone, and the intense productivity expectations, I was having panic attacks daily and struggled to avoid switching. I wasn't sure how much longer I could do the job.

Then covid hit. The world watched as people were dying at an alarming rate due to this virus that ran rampant throughout the world. No one was safe. Morgues were overrun and bodies were piling up in refrigerator trucks behind hospitals. Every person was locked in their house and were avoiding the outside because of a literal plague.

Lockdowns were not isolated to individual people. Entire companies were adjusting. We were all moved home with a laptop, a computer screen, a bunch of cords, a mouse, and a keyboard. As it turned out, working from home was so good for me and my mental health. I was able to have peace and quiet as I focused on my work, and my dog was there to keep me calm in the stressful moments.

Up until May of 2020, my brain hadn't made a new alter since my system came out of dormancy in 2019. That all changed when I was sitting on my couch watching a YouTube video of George Floyd being murdered by Minneapolis police. The scene was not far from where I had previously lived. As I watched the life drifting out of Mr. Floyd, hearing his cries for his mom, I felt my body grow cold, my mind went muddy, and I began to float away – a feeling that I came to realize was my brain making a new alter.

This was the moment that the reality of an insidious racial injustice in our country came to the forefront for me and millions of other Americans. Up until this point, so many people did not see or understand the inequity that our black and brown citizens were facing. It became more and more apparent as black person after black person was being murdered by police. By the very people that were hired to keep us all safe.

I admit that I was ignorant. I had been so sheltered in my life that I believed that slavery was over and that racial inequality and inequity were not so much of an issue anymore. I was wrong, and I began taking action to educate myself and become an ally and advocate.

It was also at this time that the veil was taken from my eyes and I saw the modern Evangelical movement for what it was, a money-making alt right façade. The indoctrination of young children all the way to adulthood was abhorrent to me. To think that I had been hurt so badly by an organization and still defended them was embarrassing.

This offshoot of mainstream Christianity was full of people who were saying they love all people, but would then turn their backs on the homeless and destitute in our population. People who were pro-life, but only until birth, because after that, you need to 'pull yourself up by the bootstraps'. People who demonized addicts and the mentally ill and would put their own family out if it meant that their image was on the line.

It was so very clear to me that the Evangelical church was no longer about Jesus, but about feeling righteous and justified in their 'sins' that hurt so many people. Jesus would be appalled at the modern church. He taught that we are supposed to love the least of these, to feed the hungry, and help out the poor. He stood for love, peace, patience, and kindness. He would never have turned his back on a homeless person, shamed an addict, or turned away someone seeking safety for them and their families.

With all of this change and unrest, I found that I was becoming increasingly torn between who I used to be as an alter, who I was ideologically, and who I was becoming. Growing is a part of life, and as long as I was moving forward, I knew I was going to be okay, but it was a very uncomfortable time.

ANNIKA ROSE

Growth and Success

Ages 37-39

While I don't remember a lot of 2021 and 2022, I do know that I was promoted once more to the highest level of claims, which was my goal from the day I was hired.

In therapy, we began to work more on the trauma that each alter had experienced. My therapist worked with whatever alter was out during therapy. She validated our experiences, encouraged our growth, and consoled the grief that many of us struggled with.

I remembered that I had written my whole trauma story in 2016 and we began to go through it. At some point in 2022, Annika began to write this book, using each chapter to process trauma and gain a clearer view of what our body had actually been through. Up until this point, we knew we had a lot of traumas, but didn't realize the frequency and extent to which we were impacted.

I was terrified of anyone finding out that I had DID. I was convinced that I would never be loved again, that I could lose my job, and be shunned from my family. It turned out that none of these things were the truth.

First, I made a couple of friends who became bonus sisters. When they found out that I had DID, their first reaction was to the effect of "Well, there is just more of you to love". As I became comfortable with them, I was able to drop the mask and let them witness my switching. There were no repercussions, rather, they were so supportive, and it became a non-issue.

Next, I found it important to tell my manager at work about the diagnosis because there was a very real risk that I could get deposed in lawsuits because of the nature of my job. I knew that I would not be able to be a credible witness and I would not be able to go through that stress without switching. I approached him, filled with fear. As I told him, his face softened and his first statement to me was, "How can we support you?".

While I gathered proof that I was not an abomination, I noticed that I was not the only person who struggled with these feelings. I noticed on social media that other systems existed and struggled with the same fears, and that there were SO many people who were grossly misinformed on the diagnosis.

I decided that the only way to combat the misinformation around DID was to create a platform where I could teach about the disorder by sharing my story and supporting others with the same struggles. In September of 2022, I made the leap and came out on social media as having dissociative identity disorder. This decision was pivotal in my growth and healing, as well as in the writing of this book.

My system was finally secure financially, physically, emotionally, and mentally, and started to see rapid growth in our life. We began looking for a house at the end of 2022, and was able to purchase one in the spring of 2023. This is also when our social media following rapidly increased as we educated about the disorder on livestreams and helped people struggling with DID to feel seen and heard.

Once we found reliable safety, we soared from goal to goal. Working full time, writing this book, building relationships, and buying a house are just a few of the accomplishments that I never thought were in the cards for me. We have deconstructed from the toxic Christianity that we were involved with, and have found our spirituality within the Universe that supports us.

Honestly, if you had asked me on the night that I was sobbing on the air mattress if we would be here, I would have laughed in your face.

Having DID can be debilitating, and we struggle every day with our job, our activities of daily living, and with remembering to show up to appointments. However, the more we work with our therapist to process our traumas, the more we prove to ourselves and others that you can live through immense trauma and come out on the other side.

No matter what you have gone through, what diagnosis you have, or the circumstances that you now live in, it's important to know that you can go from surviving to thriving. It is possible, as long as you wake up each day and choose care, compassion, and commitment to yourself and to your healing.

After years of despair and suicidality, I am excited to say that this is not where my story ends… it's where it continues… it's where it gets better.

ANNIKA ROSE

APPENDIX A

About My System

As of publishing, my system is thriving. We have about 19 alters that we know of, all with some degree of dissociative amnesia between them. Some of my alters don't have contact with any other alters, and some of my alters have communication with multiple others. For instance, Hailey has some communication with 29, 5, Annika (me), and a limited amount of communication with 35. I have the unique ability to connect in one way or another with every alter, which is the only way that this book could be written.

As I mentioned in the beginning of the book, each of my alters have their own full identity, including likes, dislikes, preferences, range of emotion, temperament, roles in the system, etc. Some have traditional names, and others are named with a number, which is their age.

Note about hosts: Every part that has a number was a host at some point. Sometimes when another part is created, that host stays put at their age and the next alter takes over the hosting role.

These are the alters in my system as of publishing in 2024:

"Little Sister": She is about 3 years old and holds the need for nurturing and safe physical touch. She often cries and is mute if she fronts.

"5": She is 5 years old and is everyone's favorite alter. She embodies sunshine, delight, wonder, and innocence. Loves tiaras, anything princess related, unicorns, and making people happy.

"Alex": She is 8 years old. She is the protector of the 'littles' and is also a trauma holder. She was created to handle the punishments at the daycare provider's house.

"Hush": She is around 8 years old, is a trauma holder and holds the fear of being heard and being in the way. She feels the most comforted while hiding under blankets and pillows – especially when talking to someone.

"Jade": She is 14 years old and is the epitome of 'angsty teenager'. She doesn't know why she is in a system and would rather not be.

"16": She is 16 years old and is in high school. Not much is known about her other than the fact that she is highly self-conscious about the body and is dabbling with the eating disorder behaviors.

"19": She is 19 years old, is in college, and is a devout 'Born-Again Christian'. She is a bit judgy, severely anorexic, and has high body dysmorphia.

"21": She is 21 years old, is deeply in love with Ian, and is very concerned with being what Ian wants. Her focus is fulfilling the 'Good Christian Wife' role.

"The In-Betweens": These are 3 alters that are around the age of 24. Not much is known about them other than one of their names is "Charlotte". They got us through our marriage to Ian. Hailey does not have much memory of this time in our life.

"26": She is 26 years old and was created when the divorce occurred. She handled treatment for the eating disorder and mastered DBT (dialectical behavior therapy) all while starting college again and dealing with the many physical ailments that the body faced. Her role in the system right now is unknown, however she does come out every now and then.

"29": She is 29 years old, was created during the strip search at the Dallas treatment center, and was solidified during the rape that occurred a month after treatment ended. (We were technically 30 when 29 was created, however, her name remains "29".) She now acts as the protector of the system.

"35": She is 35 years old, was created in the airport on the way to treatment in Arizona. She is mainly recovered from the eating disorder and is in a good place. She likes to clean and organize and is very creative as far as arts and crafts are concerned. She comes out on Sundays for our "Sunday Reset" to get ready for the week ahead.

"Present Hailey": She was created while watching the murder of George Floyd. She took over the hosting role and helped write the last part of the book and also edited the whole book to verify that what was in it was appropriate to share. She works, pays the bills, dates, and does other 'normal' activities. She is pretty close to what we would look like if we did not have DID.

"Annika Rose": ME! I was created to handle the stress of writing our trauma story and this book. I do not know exactly how old I am; however, I think I am in my upper 30's. I don't have any of my own trauma so it was easy-ish for me to write the traumas and support the different parts in their exploration of their own traumas.

"Sasha": She is in her upper 30's and was created in 2020 when we found out a boyfriend of 10 months had been married the whole time. She told the wife what was happening and said goodbye to the cheating SOB. She is now our highly energetic, party-loving, less inhibited part. She has none of her own trauma and has a hard time understanding why we need boundaries if we are having fun.

"Janelle": She was created in the airport in 2022 when our system was too overwhelmed to navigate the Christmas madness. She now comes out whenever we are in airports.

"The Angry Part": The name speaks for itself. This part is masculine in nature and only affects us on the inside with cruel inner thoughts that are aimed mainly at Hailey. This part never fronts, except to work with our therapist very sparingly.

Our system is likely not done making new alters, but we have gotten very good at adapting and adjusting to any shifts that our brain makes to cope with this life.

It's also important to note that we go by Hailey in public – no matter which part is fronting. DID is not meant to be an overt disorder as it was created to protect us. On an average day, the only way you would know which part is fronting is if you were someone we trust and someone that we know accepts our DID.

APPENDIX B

FAQ

Q: How many alters do you have in your system

A: At the time of publication, we have around 19 alters. We know this because we have worked with our therapist, mapped it out in journals, and have heard from friends about different parts that have surfaced.

Q: Can you drive? What if a little comes out when you are driving?

A: Yes, we can drive. After a lot of work in therapy we have been able to create boundaries and rules within our system. Our littles do not come out while we are driving. As a matter of fact, our littles only come out when they feel safe – and that would not be while we are driving.

Q: Can you work? What if you switch while you are working?

A: Yes, Hailey works. It is definitely difficult, but she does a fantastic job balancing the stresses of the job with our mental health. If she switches during the work day, the alter that came out will step away from the computer and get grounded so Hailey can come out again. Luckily, that doesn't happen often.

Q: Do you have any males in your system?

A: No, as of publishing, we only have female alters.

Q: Who is the 'original' alter?

A: There is no 'original' alter, as DID is the brain's inability to create one cohesive personality in early childhood, which gives the appearance of multiple identities. Just like if you drop a bowl and it shatters and I tell you to pick up the original bowl, could you? No, because all the pieces are a part of the whole.

Q: Did you have any idea that you had DID before you were diagnosed? What did you think was happening?

A: I did not have any idea that I had DID before diagnosis in 2014. There were a few doctors that tossed out the idea as early as 2009, but I vehemently denied it. I just thought I had bad memory and that people were mistaking me for other people.

Q: Do you think DID is accurately represented in the media?

A: Absolutely not. Hollywood likes to sensationalize it and make it seem dangerous, which it is not.

Q: Will you keep making alters throughout your life?

A: Likely. When I was diagnosed, I only had 8 alters that we knew about. Now we have 19 or so.

Q: Can you have non-human alters?

A: I have heard of other systems having non-human alters, so I know it can happen, it is just not something that we have experienced.

Q: Is integration the gold-standard for healing?

A: This is an outdated view of healing for people with DID. There are many ways that someone can live with, and heal from, DID. My goal is to be as healthy as possible, whatever that means for my system. I assume it will be "Functional Multiplicity" which just means we live a happy, healthy, productive life WITH our alters.

Q: What if alters don't get along with each other?

A: This can happen. Imagine having 19 different people in one house, permanently. Things are bound to get tense. The nice thing is that they are separated for the most part and don't interact with all the other parts.

Q: Are you afraid of your system/are you dangerous?

A: Absolutely not. While each part has their own identity and behavior, there are none of my parts that are dangerous. It is also important to note that I have not met one system that has been inherently dangerous. This misconception comes from the sensationalism of Hollywood.

Q: How can one support a friend or family member if they have DID?

A: Ask them directly how you can best support them. So many times, people will try to anticipate the needs and triggers of their loved one and then either try to control the environment, or step on eggshells to avoid any issues. People with DID have often had their control taken away and have been subjected to extensive nervous-system altering events. It is important that they feel somewhat in control of their surroundings in order to feel a sense of safety. You cannot predict their triggers and needs, so just ask them what they need from you. Put the ball in their court so they can coach you on how to support them.

ANNIKA ROSE

APPENDIX C

The Treatment Timeline

Throughout my life I have engaged with many different treatment styles and therapies, some which were immensely helpful, and some that did not resonate as much. Regardless of the type of therapy, I was able to use the skills that each one taught me to build the foundation upon which I stand now. Had I not given my all to each therapy, I do not believe that I would be as highly functioning as I am. Something that I wish everyone knew when they went into therapy or treatment is that it is not the therapy or treatment center that makes or breaks your recovery, it is how you work the different skills and programs that will move you forward in your journey.

As a caveat, I am aware of what a privilege it is to have health care that covers these treatments and therapies. In the United States, healthcare is not universal yet which causes major barriers to care for millions of people. I am grateful that I have had the opportunity to benefit from all of the following therapies:

2000: Outpatient eating disorder treatment for bulimia. I attended singular outpatient appointments with my parents, as I was still a minor.

2003: Outpatient therapy in college.

2004: Partial inpatient eating disorder treatment for anorexia. This was 8-12 hours of monitored care consisting of psychoeducational groups, Cognitive

Behavioral Therapy (CBT), art therapy, talk therapy, dietician appointments, and doctor appointments, as well as supervised meals and snacks. I did this for 4 weeks before Ian convinced me to stop so we could save money.

2009 June: Admitted to the psych/medical floor at the hospital due to the conversion disorder, depression, and anxiety.

2009 July: Inpatient eating disorder treatment for anorexia. This was 24/7 support including all of the elements of partial inpatient treatment, supplemented with more individualized care in order to heal the body enough to engage fully with other therapies.

2009 August: Stepped down from inpatient to partial inpatient treatment. Here, I was diagnosed with PTSD which added to my growing list of diagnosis. I was misdiagnosed with Borderline Personality Disorder (BPD) while my treatment team was discussing the possibility of a Dissociative Identity Disorder (DID) diagnosis. At this time, I was vehemently against the DID diagnosis. This was also the beginning of my Dialectical Behavior Therapy (DBT) journey that would last for 5 years.

2010 January: Stepped back up into inpatient treatment for anorexia, PTSD, anxiety, depression, and conversion disorder.

2010 February: Transferred from inpatient treatment which focused on the medical side of the eating disorder to residential treatment which focused equally on the behavioral side and the medical side of the disorder.

2010 February – April: Stepped down from residential treatment to partial inpatient when my insurance deemed me medically stable enough to do so – against my provider's wishes. (This is when Ian informed me that we were getting a divorce.) We noticed that my trauma was the real problem, and the eating disorder was secondary, so we began Eye Movement Desensitization and Reprocessing (EMDR) therapy. Eventually, I continued to step down to intensive outpatient treatment which was 3-4 hours per day with one supervised snack and one supervised meal, along with 1-2 groups.

2010 May: Finally, I stepped down into outpatient treatment which consisted of one doctor appointment, dietician appointment, and individual therapy appointment, as well as a DBT class and therapy session. This lasted until 2012.

2012-2014: Discharged from eating disorder treatment and continued to 1 individual therapy appointment per week with an outside therapist. We worked on the PTSD primarily.

2014 August: Admitted myself into trauma treatment in Dallas where they discovered that I was misdiagnosed with BPD, and was subsequently diagnosed with DID. During the 23 days that I was admitted, I learned about the effect that my trauma had on my brain, as well as the complexity of my system. At this point I had 8 alters and began to write my trauma timeline as much as I could remember it. Treatment here was much more intense than the treatment for the eating disorder. Therapy was 2, sometimes 3 hours long and consisted of intentionally triggering different alters in order to map the system and learn to get a handle on it.

2014 September: I went through 8 therapists who all told me that they were not well versed in DID and that they were not able to treat me.

2014 October: The "Healing" on Halloween when my system went dormant due to the lack of safety I experienced in the church. I stopped therapy all together until 2018 when I was finding it very difficult to cope with my everyday life.

2018: Began DBT again at a dedicated DBT clinic. Each round of the therapy was 6 months. I went through 2 rounds.

2019 March: Admitted myself to Sierra Tucson for DID, PTSD, anorexia, anxiety, and depression. This was by far the safest I had felt in *years*. Here I was exposed to treatments I had not yet experienced including inner child work, biofeedback, acupuncture, meditation, and equine therapy. This was definitely the turning point in my mental health journey

2019 May: Stepped down to intensive outpatient treatment once I moved to my new city and got settled in.

2019 July - Present: Began outpatient therapy 2 times per week utilizing narrative therapy mainly, along with traditional talk therapy.

2022: Residential eating disorder treatment for 3 days at a treatment facility that should have been shut down a long time ago.

In all, I have had treatment for my mental health for the entirety of my adult life and am not ashamed of it at all. I found the most effective therapies for me were narrative therapy (writing this book and processing it as I went), and just building safety with my providers.

I have learned so much about myself, about how to navigate difficult situations, and about the trauma that caused the DID. I've learned to radically accept that this is the way that my brain works, and I've built the bravery to share my story in order to help others feel seen, heard, and understood.

My treatment is not over, and in some ways, I feel like it is just beginning. I am finally stable financially, physically, and emotionally and can start working toward functional multiplicity – where my system can live a happy, healthy, productive life with DID.

~~~

TRIGGER WARNING

ANNIKA ROSE

TRIGGER WARNING

Made in United States
North Haven, CT
01 June 2024

53203189R00136